KATE
LANGFORD

HAVE YOUR CAKE
and EAT IT TOO

A MODERN BUSINESSWOMAN'S GUIDE TO SUCCESS

"Kate Langford is such an amazing lady. Kate encourages women like myself that they are capable of reaching their goals and dreams. Somehow Kate's words give you strength to face life's challenges. Her ambitions are infectious. She is such a caring, loving, compassionate person who genuinely has your best interests at heart. Kate is an absolute inspiration to us all."

– Cheryl Clark

"I am so glad I contacted Kate and had a one hour consult with her. She was very friendly, professional and asked me the right questions to get to know my personality type as well as my skills and experience. She was straight to the point and helped me come up with a plan and gave me the clarity and motivation I needed. I would recommend Kate's services."

– Elly Heairfield

"Kate's experience speaks for itself. In just a single hour business consult, I gained so much more clarity around the next steps in my business. It was almost like a rapid-fire session: constant dialogue, ideas and insights with clear actions as well, almost like little fireworks going off. I left the session feeling more focused, clear and inspired with my business. Highly recommended."

– Renee Zaia

"I highly recommend Kate Langford Career Consulting, especially the Career Accelerator course, for anyone wanting to get clear on their professional direction. Each coaching session was positive, constructive and I felt really listened to. The training modules were fantastic, easy to work through, and having it for life - fantastic! I can see myself going back and rewatching in the future. This is a team of fabulous people who really care about their clients!"

– Kate Barnett

"Kate Langford is always looking after the needs of others in a positive and knowledgeable way. Caring and has so much down to earth wisdom to guide you through in the right direction."

– Justine Easton

"Oh my goodness! I couldn't have asked for any better! It's fantastic. You have given me back the confidence I needed to kick start my new journey. I am now more excited than ever to get myself out there and make a difference! Thank you so much for all you do."

– Meredith Dorham

"Kate is one of the most talented and inspirational people in this field. Her passion and commitment to ensuring you achieve your success is the beyond any expectations. Thank you for putting me on my path to success."

– Kym Levy

Have Your Cake and Eat It Too: A modern businesswoman's guide to success

© Kate Langford 2023
www.katelangford.com.au
ask@katelangford.com.au

This book reflects the author's present recollections of experiences over time. Some names and characteristics have been changed, some events have been compressed, and some dialogue has been recreated.

Please note that I don't make any guarantees about the results of the information applied in this book. I share educational and informational resources that are intended to help you succeed in starting your own business. You nevertheless need to know that your ultimate success or failure will be the result of your own efforts, your particular situation, and innumerable other circumstances beyond my knowledge and control.

This book is sold with the understanding that the author is not offering specific personal advice to the reader. For specific professional advice, seek the services of Kate Langford Career Consulting or Kate Langford Business Consulting. The author disclaims any responsibility for liability, loss or risk, personal or otherwise, that happens as a consequence of the use and application of any of the contents of this book.

All rights reserved. This book may not be reproduced in whole or part, stored, posted on the internet, or transmitted in any form or by any means, electronic, mechanical, photocopying, recording, or other, without permission from the author of this book.

Self published by Kate Langford with edit, design, and publishing support by Clark & Mackay

ISBN: 978-1-922784-67-4 (Paperback)

A catalogue record for this book is available from the National Library of Australia

This is dedicated to my grandfather, David Lawson, who was a writer.
I am so proud to be carrying on your legacy.
And to *you*, the modern businesswoman.
Put down your battle sword, because you no longer have to fight to nail everything in life.
Yes, you *can* have it all, but from this day forward,
it will be with ease and flow.
You are seen. You are loved. You are heard.
I've got you.
Go get it!

CONTENTS

Chapter 1: Strap In...1
Chapter 2: Drive 9
Chapter 3: Flexibility 23
Chapter 4: Family 33
Chapter 5: Business... 47
Chapter 6: Time... 61
Chapter 7: Self-Worth 73
Chapter 8: Money 85
Chapter 9: Growth 95
Chapter 10: Health 109
Chapter 11: Resilience 123
Chapter 12: Love... 141
Chapter 13: Balance 161
Chapter 14: Vision 171
Chapter 15: Guidance 185

About the Author... 201
Kate Langford Career Consulting 204
Kate Langford Business Consulting 207
Acknowledgments.. 211

CHAPTER 1
STRAP IN...

*W*hat... the... heck!

It was all I could think as the wind rushed past me. There I was, strapped to an experienced tandem skydiving master, free-falling after jumping out of a plane at 10,000 feet. This guy had done this hundreds, maybe thousands, of times before, but this time was different.

As the ground got closer and closer, I could feel him rustling around behind me. Everyone else who had jumped before and after us had already deployed their parachutes and were gliding around having the time of their lives.

We were still falling.

"Are we okay?" I managed to ask as the wind continued to whip at my face.

"No, the chute is not opening," came his matter-of-fact reply as he worked frantically to cut the primary parachute from our harnesses.

He hacked through the thick straps with a knife, and I watched on with a combination of horror and awe as our parachute drifted away so delicately from us, leaving two thick wires sticking out of our harness.

Is this how I'm going to die?

Even now, I am surprised that I didn't panic at the thought. Maybe it was an oversupply of adrenaline, stark denial, or pure shock, but the realisation that I was facing off with death itself was not enough to make my heart race or my palms sweat. There was a complete sense of calm, even though I was looking straight down as the ground felt like it was rushing up to meet us. I didn't freak out or scream or carry on; I went to a place of complete surrender.

I don't live with regrets; I don't believe in doing that. Every day that I am fortunate enough to wake up, I do what I say I'm going to do and say exactly what I need to say. I show up as I am and never pretend. If I was going to die that day, I knew I would not have anything I wished I had said or done. I was ready whenever my time was up.

"I'm going to try the secondary chute!" my tandem master called out.

By that stage, we were just two hundred metres from the ground.

"Lift your legs! Lift your legs!"

I tried my best, but the harness was so tight and the force of the wind rushing against me was so heavy that I couldn't follow the order. The chute opened with a swift *whoosh*, and I felt relief from some of that pressure instantly.

There was no time for a joyride glide; gravity was sucking us down, and it was only a matter of seconds before we hit the ground. The tandem skydiver landed right on top of me, and I took the full impact of both of us.

I sat up in a daze, not really comprehending that my ankle was jutting out at a very unnatural angle. I'd find out later that it had snapped in several places.

I'm alive!

I have no idea what happened between then and landing up in hospital. Media crews arrived before the ambulance and started rolling cameras as I sat on a large patch of grass in my maroon State of Origin jersey. You can still find online video footage taken by a local news station that shows me puffing on the green whistle given to me by the paramedics as if it were my only source of life.

My sister told me later that I was laughing with the delirium of a crazed person. I can only put that down to shock. I don't remember being in pain. When people asked if I was okay, I would dismiss their concern with "Oh, I will be alright!" There is no doubt I was loaded up on adrenaline and running in survival mode.

My accident made headlines around Australia, and it was definitely a birthday I would never forget. It was almost my thirtieth year on earth, and I had always wanted to go skydiving. I've been a goal-oriented person for as long as I can remember, and if something is on my list of goals, it's going to get crossed off come hell or high water. I had it in my head that I would skydive before I turned thirty, and I was on holiday in Cairns with my sister when I decided it was time to take the plunge.

When I set my mind to something, it happens. I was so freakin' excited, but when the day arrived, something shifted in me. I felt worried about how tight my harness was, and when the plane took off, I felt scared as hell. I was uneasy and nervous, not excited and pumped like I thought I would be. I'd had visions of jumping out at 10,000 feet with a triumphant "Hell yeah!" and loving every second of it.

None of that had happened.

Once at hospital, I went through a four-hour surgery to put pins and screws into my ankle to hold it in place. With five days confined to a hospital bed, I had a lot of time to think about how close I had been to taking my last breath. If I was a go-getter before, this near-death experience on 22 July 2012 shook me up even more to suck life dry. It was like I had been gifted a second chance, and there was no way I was going to waste a moment.

I was already a seize-the-day kinda gal before the accident, but it was now amplified tenfold. At any instant, my time could be up; that is the nature of life. As cliche as it may sound, that accident and near-death experience made me who I am today. Although a decade has passed since, if I were to die tomorrow, I wouldn't have one regret. I continue to live each day as if it were my last, and I leave nothing on the table. Most of all, I show up in each and every moment being unapologetically my authentic self.

You only get one life, so why not smash it?

A few months after the accident, I built my first home in Mackay by channelling all of my hard-earned money into my first asset. I also met the love of my life and started a family within a few years of the accident. It was like my focus was even stronger, and I just went after what I wanted with more determination.

I am now the successful owner of a million-dollar business with a second already starting to flourish.

As you will find out, I've been through my share of challenges. But then again, you would have, too. The difference between where I am now and where I could have ended up is that I never let any challenges slow me down for too long. I have honed resilience and pushed onwards and upwards after every stumble.

I get really pissed off when people say, "I can't go on, I've been through too much," or "I'm too tired to keep going," or worst of all, "I don't have time." My fight for life and drive comes from lack of patience, I'm sure of it, but it also comes from an inner desire to make the best of what I have with the time that I have. How could you waste such a precious gift with excuses?

This book is not for the excuse-makers, or the people I call "gonnas". As in, "I'm gonna make that phone call," or "I'm gonna change jobs because this one isn't right for me," or "I've always wanted to start a business; I'm gonna do it one day."

If the word "gonna" – or "going to" if you are a little more eloquent – has ever come out of your mouth, you can put this book down right now. I'm not interested in excuses or in people who are prepared to leave their dreams up in the clouds. I am all about the "doer", the person who says they are going to do something and just gets in and fucking does it.

If the idea of having your cake and eating it too is appealing, the very first step you have to take is to ban "gonna" from your vocabulary. Ban it from your very *being*. It simply cannot exist. You can't just sit back, kick up your heels, and hope that your powers of manifestation will magically bring it all into being. To have a successful life, you are going to have to roll your sleeves up and do the work!

This book is for you if you are determined to prove to the world, just like I was, that you can have it all. And by "have it all", I don't mean that you have to ace the shit out of every single component of your life every moment of every day. Not only is that physically and emotionally impossible, but even if you do manage to hit your own level of perfection, it simply is not sustainable to carry that on for the rest of your life.

So, let's get real! I am not about pushing shit uphill until you burn yourself out. If that happens, you are no good to anyone and will never be able to truly enjoy everything you have worked for.

Having it all means not discounting any area of your life. You *can* have young children and start a million-dollar business. You *can* have precious time for yourself and still nurture your relationship with your partner. You *can* wear all the hats and still have balance in your life.

Having it all means you are connected with yourself so you know which areas of your life require more attention at any given moment and you have the discipline to move from one space to another with presence and full focus so you are not multitasking and half-arsing life.

Having it all means being ready to roll up your sleeves and jump into the trenches to do whatever needs to be done so that when you have time to rest, you can be free to enjoy the fruits of your labour.

> *Sounds simple, right?*
> *So why do we make it so hard for ourselves?*

I think it is absolute bullshit that, in this day and age, women are still being pressured to choose between having a career and having a family. My goal is to shine a light on the fact that it is possible for women to have both. What's more, you don't have to be working your arse off for someone else in a corporate world where you aren't valued.

You can switch careers to something that lights you up or go out on your own, work confidently within your area of expertise, charge good money to do so, and stay in your genius zone. You can merge lifestyle with business. Leaving a corporate job and starting my own jam was my secret to having it all, and I want to give as many people the tools to achieve that as possible.

Choosing this path is by no means the bloody easy road. It is a path that will challenge you and requires you to be open to a lot of personal and professional growth. You have to work towards being able to stand at the mirror and look yourself in the eye without flinching. You have to be willing to step out of the safety of your comfort zone and take every opportunity that presents itself. You need to be driven by passion and understand the value of risk versus reward.

But don't worry. I'm not going to throw you to the wolves here. I'm not going to sit up here on a high horse and wag my finger at you, telling you what you should and shouldn't do to have it all. I am going to be in the trenches with you. I had to learn all of this the hard way, and that is why I wrote *Have Your Cake and Eat It Too:* so you can cut through the bullshit of making the same mistakes I did, learn from my experience, and fly. I've got you.

This book shares the story of how I built a million-dollar business starting with zero dollars and with two children under the age of three. It also includes some gold nugget coaching that you can get stuck into *right now* so you can build your own momentum and start seeing results.

I'm not superhuman; I'm just like you. If you are prepared for the journey, you *can* have it all, too.

CHAPTER 2
DRIVE

My brain has always worked in a way that made me feel different. Even from a young age, I have been able to connect the dots faster than the average human. When a problem is presented to me, all of the possible solutions light up in my mind, like the guy on *The Good Doctor*.

My brain works so fast that sometimes I can't even keep up, but it has never worked for me in an academic sense. I had a C-grade average, so I was never what you would consider book-smart intelligent. But I had an emotional intelligence that was through the roof. My mind could connect the dots in real-life situations based off verbal cues and body language at lightning speed. It's a different smart.

It's almost impossible to describe, but it's as if this whole web of possibilities lights up in my mind, and there are always multiple options for any given situation. It happens faster than I can even verbalise it most of the time. From there, I have all of the options laid out, and it is a process of elimination and priority for me to decide which is the first action to take to reach a solution. If that doesn't work, I already have the second lined up.

Sounds fantastic, doesn't it? But let me tell you, a hyper-analytic brain comes with heightened emotions, and it has been a lifelong process of learning how to channel it and how to handle it in a way that helps me.

Dad was an entrepreneur long before the word became cool. I watched him try his hand at a few things, like selling shade sails and operating a pie van as I was growing up. It planted the very early seeds of what is possible when you take control of your own life, and I remember running a street-side lemonade stall and selling toys for five cents to make myself some pocket money.

Even still, I never backed myself as an entrepreneur until I started Above and Beyond Resumes in 2015. I would run other people's businesses with great success, but the thought of doing it myself scared me until that point. But Dad always had a saying: "No matter what you do, be the best at it," and I ran with it. He'd follow it up with, "Even if you are a garbage truck driver, you've just got to be the best damn garbage truck driver there is."

Although I was never the best at English or Math, I was awesome at sports. I was a cross-country runner, and I played state representative netball and touch football for Metropolitan North and competed in Little Athletics at the Queensland state titles for discus. I travelled around the country for various sports and loved every moment of it.

I also had the best emotional intelligence of anyone in my class. It allowed me to navigate just about any situation in my young life and come out winning. I can read people. I always remember noticing one of my high school teachers showing up one day for class and her behaviour had changed. She had a weird combination of enthusiasm and weariness, and her hands seemed to linger around her stomach a lot more than they had before. Yes, I notice these things. Towards the end of class, I raised my hand. "Are you pregnant, miss?" She was speechless – and likely a little pissed off at me – but she nodded her head as the class erupted in applause.

> I know intuition and perception are my superpowers, and they are excellent skills to have as a career and business coach.

It means I can sniff out bullshit in less than five minutes and can always tell if people are being shifty or inauthentic, which grinds my gears.

I graduated high school with an OP (Overall Position – a ranking system used to determine which university courses you could apply for) of 14. The lowest was 25. I was relieved that school was finished, because I was tired of trying to shape the way my brain operated to fit the way it was "supposed" to, as the teachers expected of me. I didn't think the way everyone else did, and it made the traditional public school system hard for me to tackle.

I remember bumping into my accounting teacher at the high school formal, and she said, "Kate, you're going to be something one day, and you don't even realise it. You think differently. Don't underestimate the power of what you're going to be in life."

She made me feel seen. I had spent many frustrated lunchtimes sitting in her classroom trying my bloody hardest to wrap my head around the latest economic concept she was trying to teach me. I laugh at how, a quarter of a decade later, I can use software to do my business profit and loss statements, and I don't really need to know the minute details of how it is done after all. It suits a big-picture thinker like me perfectly fine!

Although school was a challenge for me, I couldn't wait to start work. Before I had reached the minimum allowable age to start work in Australia at the time – fourteen years and nine months – I had written my first résumé. Dad rang the local Domino's pizza franchise and talked me up. "Kate is one of the best workers you will ever meet!"

The manager asked Dad to bring me down with my résumé. The day after we dropped it in, I got a call with an offer of a role as a window washer with the opportunity to help with some customer service duties. I jumped at it. I was prepared to be the best fucking window washer they had ever seen.

Never satisfied with just showing up and doing my work, I was a high achiever even back then and wouldn't settle on being *così così*, which is Italian for so-so. It is a phrase I didn't learn until my two eldest children went to primary school, but it is the perfect way to describe my approach to everything I do. I never wanted to have a *così così* life, and that included what I did for work.

Domino's used to have badges that staff could earn for completing certain tasks, and my hat was full of them. I was the leader of the pack in our store. I had moved from window washer to customer service operator to pizza cutter to pizza maker. When I reached the stage where I could make the pizza, I learned about the badges for that section. You could be timed on how quickly you could make a Supreme Pizza – because that was the one that has the most toppings. There was a bronze, silver, gold, platinum, and the highest level had wings on it. *Well, if the wings are the highest, I'm going to get that!*

I kept training so I could get faster and faster, and I was the main pizza-maker on Friday, Saturday, and Sunday nights. I became so good at it, the manager pulled me aside and said, "Kate, you should enter this national competition! The best of the best enter, and they give you an official time."

I was nervous as hell. Even though I would enter as part of a team from our store, the thought of all eyes being on me when it was my turn to step up to the table and compete was enough to make me hesitate a little. But there was a stronger voice inside me that cut through the instinct to refuse and not be seen. *I have to give it a go!* It's a conflict I have experienced many times since, but every single time without fail, I take those nerves and harness them. It is a sign that whatever is about to come is going to push me out of my comfort zone, and that's a place I hate staying for too long.

"Never say no to an opportunity" is a motto that has served me well in life, and I am so grateful that I knew that in my bones even as a teenager. Everyone gets nervous at some stage in their lives, but when you push through, that's when you grow. That's when you expand. That's when you can say you've taken a dive into the coldest metaphorical water you can imagine and, once you've done it, shout out, "Oh my God, that was bloody invigorating!"

Whenever I feel those nerves chomping at my heels, I know I'm about to launch into something great. At that particular time, it was a national pizza-making competition. My team stood to the side cheering, "Gooooooo Kate!" as I took my position on the pizza line.

The buzzer went off, and I flew into action. *Grab the dough, sauce it, slide the base onto the maker, sixty grams cheese base, thirty grams pepperoni, thirty grams capsicum, thirty grams onion, thirty grams beef, thirty grams pineapple, sixty grams cheese, thirty grams bacon sprinkled on top, pat it down, take the ring off and slide it into the oven and hit the buzzer.*

Turns out, I was one of the fastest Domino's Supreme Pizza makers in the country and could create a perfect Supreme Pizza in 16.1 seconds, which included literally weighing every ingredient so it fit national standards. Our store was ranked third in the country, and because I was the fastest of our crew, there was status that went with that.

I love being the best, I'm not going to lie, but as the years have passed, it's more about being the best for *me*, not being the best in other people's eyes. I acknowledge I was driven by external validation when I was younger because I didn't have a strong sense of self-worth. The way I spoke to myself about myself was not the healthiest. I believed I could do anything and always gave every opportunity a go, but I needed someone else to tell me I had nailed it in order to believe it for myself.

Thank goodness I left that way of thinking in the dust *looooong* ago! If you see this pattern in the way you talk to yourself, ask yourself, *why is that pattern there?* It's time to deal with the root cause of that so you can step into your own greatness and be unapologetically you!

When I turned seventeen, I reached my goal of becoming a manager at work. My boss was impressed by my work ethic, and I was responsible for thirty staff members, some of them being as old as thirty-eight. This was my first real crack at leadership, and I was so excited!

I instinctively led by example, and still do. On a closing shift, the floors had to be mopped, and it was the job everyone hated the most. So I would grab a mop and start on the floors with, "C'mon guys, let's get stuck in and do this." No one taught me how to do that, but when I reflect, I think it comes from a moral integrity piece. I always believed, *I'm not going to ask you to do something if I'm not prepared to do it myself.* Also, I never wanted to be a shit human. I saw my fair share of bullying at school, which I'll go into later, so I instinctively knew the best way to build a team was to be in the trenches with them, not up on some high horse like a dictator.

It wasn't all smooth sailing, of course. I felt insecure managing conflict, but I never let it beat me. There was one particular driver, Henry, who seemed to enjoy sitting out the back smoking instead of actually doing his job. If it was something in the store, I would muck in and lead by example, but as deliveries were outside of the store, I couldn't rely on that tactic. Instead, I'd try to soften it a little with something like, "You all right? I just got a heap of orders that need to go out."

I understand it wasn't direct, but I was afraid to be too strong in getting my message across. Whenever Henry was dismissive of me, I would seek advice from Helen, the owner, and she gave me confirmation of what I was within my rights to demand as a manager. With that in place, I felt more confident to back myself. The next time Henry fobbed me off, I responded with, "I know I am younger than you and that probably annoys you, but I have been put in this position, and you have a job to do, so let's just get on with it."

There will always be conflict in life, and this was my first opportunity to address it head-on in a work environment. I have maintained that pattern ever since: seek counsel, back myself, and keep going.

 I intuitively know how to handle a situation, but equally, I know that no one is beyond needing help sometimes.

Helen was my first strong female role model. When we started hanging out socially, Helen made me feel good about myself. She made me feel worthy of praise, like I was destined for great things in life. It was a very empowering connection, because I had never felt a true sense of belonging until I met Helen.

The flip side of that strong bond was that whenever we had an argument, as friends do, I would feel like my world was ending. Our relationship was strained as I struggled to actually make a decision about whether or not to stay working at the store. There was a time when I wanted to own my own store. But when I saw my future mirroring Helen's, I knew in my heart that that was not what I truly felt pulled towards. She was in her late thirties with no partner, no kids, and was hanging out with younger people in a highly stressful environment. I knew from a young age that I wanted a family. In many ways, my earliest life goal was to become a mum.

In the six months prior to leaving Domino's, I had been accepted into a Bachelor of Social Work at the Queensland University of Technology. I knew I wanted to help people, but I quickly remembered how awful schooling was. For some reason, I had pictured university as being a little freer, but it was just as committed to learning through assessment. I found the course content too constricting and didn't make it past one semester.

This removed the light at the end of the tunnel for my Domino's situation. With a degree in hand, I'd be set for a whole new career, but when I called it quits, I was back at square one. I would yo-yo between "I'll just resign and find something better" and "Oh no! I can't do it!" The indecision led to full anxiety, which is still triggered at times to this day, although I have a much better handle on it now. When I made the firm decision to leave, I knew it was the right choice. I just had to back myself and not stress about the what-ifs.

An opportunity came up to work in a government department, and I could see a career pathway of progression, flexibility, steady pay, and great benefits. Let's be honest, none of it was real, but for a naive younger me, it was enough to motivate me to take action and leave Domino's.

I excelled at my position in the call centre, but I couldn't climb the ladder. I felt completely stifled by red tape, and there was no room for creative thinking or innovative solutions. Instead, we had to do things the *only* way that was laid out for us. I lasted about a year before the stagnation got to me. Coming back to my calling to help people, I thought about recruitment and found an ad on SEEK (a job search platform) for a position that caught my attention.

Although Helen had been my first female role model, Michelle became my first mentor. Our professional relationship began when she hired me for my first role in the recruitment industry. I will never forget how her straight-to-the-point manner was able to reel in all of my expectations of what I was in for when I started working under her in 2005.

"Do you know what recruitment is based on?" she asked me during the job interview.

"Oh yeah, it's about finding the right jobs for the right people." *Nailed it!*

"Wrong. It's about sales."

I tried not to let the shock show on my face.

"Oh... right. I can probably do that."

Michelle saw something in me and took me under her wing. I started as a recruitment coordinator, which is essentially admin-based and included reference checking, calling candidates, and supporting the consultants in their work. Within six weeks, Michelle offered me a role as a consultant, directly interviewing candidates, matching candidates with clients, booking them for interviews, and keeping tabs on them once they became employed. I was surprised that I had progressed so quickly, but I also knew that I had a natural flair for dealing with clients. Even when I was a little girl, Dad would tell me I had the "gift of the gab," a natural ability to connect with and understand people quickly. I embrace that as my genius zone.

I use the term *genius zone* a lot in this book and in my coaching, because it is vital to success in anything. That heart piece is often what is missing in the businesses that don't make it outside of the first few years. I recognised what people naturally came to me for help and what I was always talking about at barbeques with family and friends. When you pause to take notice of this, you discover where your genius zone is.

Really, if your vision does not include working in your genius zone, you are missing out on the opportunity of completeness. That is where your passion lies and where you tap into the skills that come naturally to you. One of my superpowers is telling if someone is working in their genius zone or not. I can read their energy, and if they come to me with a potential business idea, I only have to listen to the words that come out of their mouth and combine that with their body language to see if it is true for them or not. If there is a disconnect, like their language is set to "convince me" mode and their body language is flat, I know they are running from something. Remember, if you are running from something, you are not going to be a successful business owner.

I'll hit them with, "Okay, so what's going on?"

"I can't hide from you, Kate."

No, you bloody can't!

If you're not in your genius zone, you may as well throw money down the toilet. But some people don't know what that is, so I can help them to uncover it. What makes me nervous is when people want to run a business but they don't know their genius, so they're probably not a business owner. It can be really hard to say to someone, because I'm shooting their escape route down, but I also know I have saved them ten years of pain or heartache. Even though my heart is hurting, my business head is going, "I saved you."

But if they are positively bubbling over with excitement, their eyes are bright, and I can feel the high energy radiating from them, they are driven by their passion because they have found their genius zone!

> ❛ It is critical for business success to work from your genius zone, full stop! ❜

I had found my genius zone in the role Michelle had given me, but it wasn't enough. I wanted more, and I was very efficient in what I did. I knew I could climb higher. A year later, I was senior consultant, and with a few more years notched up, I was managing a temp desk with eighty people. *Whatever you do, be the best at it.* I wanted that senior position so I would be seen and could feel like I was doing well. I needed verbal affirmation, with my name being brought up at meetings, followed by praise and external validation with role advancement and pay rises; I thrived on it. It was about measurement and status. It's so far removed from the person I am today, but at the time, that was my truth.

My drive and determination was nurtured by Michelle, who helped me to truly believe in myself. Until that point, I had attracted people who took advantage of me. They saw that I would do anything for them and not expect anything in return. I liked to give. The problem was, I never received. There was no balance there.

Because I was so busy pleasing everyone around me, I had not really uncovered my own identity. I had a feeling that I would be something, but no one could see me. It's like I was screaming inside, "Hey! Look! I am doing well!" Michelle was the first person who truly saw me, and I had to wait until I was twenty-three to know what that felt like. She made me feel worthy of my success and showed me what was possible. Michelle taught me that I didn't need to worry about external chatter or the opinions of others. Under her guidance, I stopped beating myself up whenever things didn't work out as I had planned.

Having something to strive for is vital to giving you direction. This is true whether you view it from a life, career, or business perspective. Mum told me that ever since I was a kid, I would write motivational things on my wall. They were my vision of goals and things that would push me through when times got tough. I have always been focused, and that has never faded. Whatever I set my mind to, I am locked and loaded and ready for action.

On the last day of my working year, right before I go on holidays, I set goals on my whiteboard for the year ahead. They could be personal or professional goals, and I choose my top five to write down on a whiteboard that I can see clearly from my desk. Not a day goes by when I don't acknowledge them and do a quick check-in with myself to see how I am tracking. Every year, the slate is wiped clean on those twelve-month goals. I may be able to celebrate achieving them, or I may have a way to go, but by the time the last working day of the year rolls around, five fresh goals go up on the board.

Gold Nuggets

At the end of each chapter, you will find Gold Nuggets; the best bits for you to take from each chapter. For more information, and to download the worksheets, please use the QR code below:

SCAN FOR

WORKSHEETS

Gold Nuggets for Drive

I have a piece of paper, which is tattered and worn, that I keep in my office that says, "Ten million in ten years." It was the very first goal I set for my business when I launched it in 2018. That goal remains in play for me, and it works because I am a visionary person. I know that where your focus goes, energy flows, and that's how you build momentum and success.

There are, of course, many more goals I set for myself. Mini goals I mentally set out to achieve each day. Every morning when I wake up, I run a quick physical and emotional scan of myself sitting in the sun with a morning Vöost (I don't drink coffee!). This is when I set some immediate goals that could be something simple, like drinking more water or taking a day to rest. For a week, I might decide that I'm going to put my feet up in the evening when the kids are in bed and watch TV with Jay rather than catching up on work, or I might commit to four gym sessions that week instead of three. For a month, it might be to get more social and connect with people so I can build my network.

All of these mini goals require future vision but also place my attention on the areas I know I need to focus on so I can be my best. My mini goals always change in priority, so while work and physical strength may be where my focus is one week, rest and emotional restoration may be the priorities the next.

Before you can set your goals, you have to determine what you value most. So grab a journal and answer the following:

- ($) List the top five things that are important to me in life.
- ($) How do I prioritise them? Number them from one, as most important, to five.
- ($) What are my three non-negotiable values as a human?
- ($) What do I want to be known for?
- ($) What do I value the most in others?
- ($) Do I know what my genius zone is?
- ($) If not, make a list of the things I am passionate about. Do they align with what I am doing in my career, or what I plan to build a business around?

CHAPTER 3
FLEXIBILITY

I fell in love for the first time when I was fifteen. Ah, young love. You remember it, right? He was perfect in my eyes and could do no wrong. He was tall, cute, athletic, charming, and best of all, he showed me attention. I literally got butterflies in my stomach when I was around him, and it wasn't long before other girls at school noticed he was interested in me. We'd be sitting in a group at lunch, and they would say, "Ooooooh, Kate! He's looking at you!"

He had a strength and masculinity that I was attracted to. I was on cloud nine when we became a couple. We hung out all the time because we had a lot of the same friends. While I had representative athletics and my own netball girls team to keep me active, we played mixed netball together, too. He played other sports throughout the year and also made it onto representative teams. As much as I was a competitor, I was also a young version of a WAG (a wife or girlfriend of a famous footballer) following him around to watch all his games.

When we graduated high school, we stayed together, and he moved into my family's house to live with me. We bought our own place together at nineteen and settled in very quickly. I really handed myself over to him and played the role of devoted girlfriend to perfection. When we'd been together for seven years, I thought the next logical step was for us to get married. I pressured him a bit to take the next step, which would get me closer to becoming the mother I had always wanted to be, and was so excited when he proposed.

At twenty-three, I had committed to the love of my young life and had a career that I loved, working with Michelle.

We had only been married for a few months when I started to feel my husband slipping away. There was a distance between us that grew larger and larger with every passing month. Then, my life changed in an instant, and I did *not* see it coming. He sat me down on our bed one night and told me he was leaving me and wanted a divorce.

One moment, I had the picture-perfect white picket fence life and we were getting ready to start a family; the next, I was moving my stuff out of our home and another woman had already begun to move her stuff in. Literally the day after I left, she was sleeping in my marital bed. It was shit, there's no way to sugar-coat it.

My heart was literally shattered into a million pieces, and he had clearly already moved on. When you are rocked to the core like that, it really makes you pause and reflect. There were some controlling behaviours that I wasn't happy about, like how, if I didn't mash a potato properly while preparing our dinner, I would cop a verbal lash, but I felt so proud to be his woman that it didn't matter to me at the time.

I am a believer in signs, you know, events that happen in a completely natural way that could easily be overlooked if you aren't paying close enough attention. There was a sign on our wedding day that I dismissed, but on reflection, it was a huge tap on the shoulder from the universe. I am very old-school and traditional, and we drove to our wedding venue in separate limos. On the way, my limo somehow ended up in front of his.

When we pulled over, I immediately looked at Mum in panic and said, "Oh no, that's a bad sign!"

She looked at me, dead serious, and asked, "Are you sure you want to get married?"

I paused to think about it. *We've been together so long. This is what we should do, right?*

"Well, we're all here now." I shrugged as the door was opened for me to step out. My mistake was basing my decision on a "should," not on what I wanted.

It was just eight months after our wedding day that everything I thought was real had been ripped away from me, like someone had stabbed my life jacket with a knife and left me to fend for myself in the middle of the ocean. I was emotionally going under and struggling to come up for air. I knew I had to rip off that useless lifejacket so I could use my arms and legs freely to save myself.

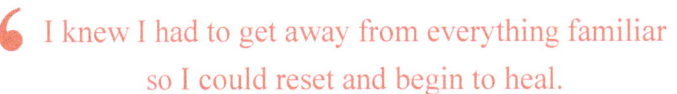

> I knew I had to get away from everything familiar so I could reset and begin to heal.

Maybe we were just too young to get married? I know that twenty-four definitely felt too young for me to be called a divorcee.

Travel had been something I'd wanted to do forever, but my ex was a homebody, so we had never been anywhere together. Since I no longer had to please him, I was free as a bird! I applied straight away for a five-year ancestry visa so I could go and live in London. This was possible as there is a fair amount of Scottish blood flowing through my veins (hence I am so white and burn to a crisp if I'm in the sun for more than ten minutes).

It was taking forever, and I was so desperate to escape that I flew down to Canberra to have the visa expedited. Six weeks after I moved out of my home, I was travelling to London on a one-way ticket. Still legally tied to the man who had now evolved into someone I didn't recognise, I made Dad my power of attorney so he could finalise my divorce and sort out the split of assets so I could literally break free.

I landed at Heathrow Airport at 4 am with nothing but my suitcase. My free spirit felt so alive, but I was scared shitless at the same time. I had no fixed accommodation, no job to go to, and didn't know a soul. I was as far out of my comfort zone as I could physically and emotionally have been at that time. I checked into the nearest hostel and went straight to the bar. I got swept up in conversation with a group of Irish guys before I realised I needed to call home to let my family know I was okay.

"I'll call your mum!" one of them bellowed.

I giggled as I handed my phone over.

"Hey, Mum! Your daughter is here with us. She's all good!"

I had no idea how Mum would have reacted to that call, which would have come around mid-afternoon in Aussie time, but at least my family knew I was safe. I relaxed into a few drinks before heading to bed once the sun came up.

The moment I woke up, I put my problem-solving hat on and worked through my immediate challenges: Place to live? *Check.* Job? *Check.* Plans to live life to the absolute bloody max? *Check.*

I was caught in the whirlwind of being in a new place with new sounds, sights, smells, and tastes, and while there was a lot of excitement during the days when I was able to explore and thrive in my new-found freedom, the nights during those first few weeks were like hell on earth for me, emotionally.

I had run halfway around the world, but there was no escaping the chest-tightening grief that had clung to me. I functioned as well as I could during the day in my role at an international company Robert Walters Recruitment. It wasn't long before I was hitting records and became the one to watch in that position as one of the top leading consultants within the London office, and it was a welcome distraction from the emotional pain that boiled away inside of me. But when the nights came and I was back in my apartment in Tooting Bec – where all of the Aussies seemed to live – I would allow myself to feel; to literally sit in the shitstorm inside my head. I would listen to sad songs and cry my eyes out. I would feel the shame of divorce and the rage at the infidelity and let it come out so it was no longer holding my mind hostage.

Where do I go from here? I'm so lonely. You are so worthless, Kate. How could you let this happen? Why didn't you see what was going on?

I went to bed exhausted every night and woke up feeling refreshed for a second or two before the weight fell back onto my chest once again every morning. *Oh, fuck! I've gotta feel this pain all over again!* I think my emotional intelligence was the only thing that prevented me from falling into full depression. I knew it would pass, but that didn't stop the excruciating pain of being in that moment in time. I took it one day at a time. Having gone through that intense emotional pain, nothing really feels hard for me anymore. It helps me to put everything into perspective.

The first three months were definitely the toughest, but little by little, that emotional weight lifted off my chest, and I began to breathe again. There were times when I would Facetime my parents and think, *What the hell am I doing all the way over here, away from my family?* I could have thrown it all in and gone back home. That would have been the easy option, but I would have robbed myself of the opportunity to change. I wanted to evolve through the grief and prove that I could back myself. I knew I wasn't done. *If I go home now, what would I have achieved? I will be the same person I was when I left.*

I chose to see it through and continue through this evolution of self. I knew it was not my natural state to be bogged down for long. My glass-half-full mindset, the one Kate Easton was renowned for, began to return. *You have a choice to stay in the shit and never be the same again, OR you can pick yourself up and realise that you are free! You can do everything you couldn't do before, you have no one to answer to but yourself!*

I had been tied to my ex-husband for so much of my life that I had forgotten how to *be* without him. My life had revolved around our routine to the point where I was expected to have dinner on the table at a certain time each night to ensure that he came home from work happy. Like a good wifey, I played my role. But now, I had to find myself all over again.

Although it was born from one of the worst moments of my life, my time overseas was by far the best experience of my life. After I rode that shitty wave of grief, I came out of my shell refreshed. It was like I had been given a blank slate. I fell instantly "in like" with myself for having the bravery to make a clean break and give myself the freedom to discover who I was. (It would be many years until I could say that I feel in *love* with myself, but since you are along for the ride, you will find out how that all panned out.)

I realised that I didn't need to *change* who I was; I just had to be comfortable with letting the real Kate out without the need for validation. I tentatively started to shed the armour I had placed around me since I was a young girl – the armour that protected me from the bullies, from the people who looked down on me or told me I was not pretty enough or smart enough. The attachment I had to making sure others liked me and the need to put on a mask to fit other people's expectations of me fell away, and I could be my authentic self, because no one around me knew who the "old" Kate was.

I made friendships, and I jumped out of my comfort zone by dating again. *I have nothing to lose!* It was the mentality I carried into everything. If I liked the look of a guy on the dancefloor, I made a move. If I wanted to visit Paris for the weekend, I booked the trip. I had never had so much freedom and fearlessness in my life.

Having never dated anyone other than my ex, I discovered who I was outside of the "power couple." I had the time of my life and have no regrets. It was part of my personal growth, developing, and understanding of what I did and didn't want in a partner.

I experienced *so* much in the two-and-a-half years I was away: I went to Oktoberfest in Germany and enjoyed steins of wine because I didn't like the taste of beer; paraglided off the Swiss Alps; explored Ireland, Scotland, Rome, Italy, France, Amsterdam, Vienna, and Paris; jumped on a Contiki bus and ran amok with some wildly fun people; celebrated my twenty-fifth birthday in Barcelona; and so much more.

I learned so much about myself. I learned how to be on my own. I learned how to rebuild myself after one of the most devastating phases of my life. I learned how to be resilient. I learned how to survive. I learned how to be free. I learned how to embrace everything about me, my fun-loving nature, my loudness, my independence, my fierceness, and my trust in myself.

I knew exactly when the time was right to come back to Australia, because I felt like I had shed the skin of the woman who felt she had to suppress herself and please others. Travelling taught me to be a doer and to never leave any opportunity on the table. If I wanted something, I had the confidence that I could go and get it. That, and my kidneys needed a break from the drinking that was essential in my London circle!

Dad managed to finalise my divorce while I was away, so when I did come home, I was free to do whatever I wanted, and I was ready to start life again.

Gold Nuggets for Flexibility

True flexibility comes when you can show up as your authentic self each and every day. This is a lesson that took me *years* to learn, and it most certainly is not resolved at this stage of the book, so I want you to draw a line in the sand right now and make a decision to never make yourself small for anyone else... ever again!

Grab your journal and write down:

- ⓢ Three times I have not spoken up because of what other people might think.

- ⓢ A time when I have gone along with something that felt wrong.

- ⓢ A time when I have done something because I felt like I *should* do it.

- ⓢ A time when I have made myself miserable because I was too afraid to ask for what I wanted.

There is a concept you will see *a lot* in this book, because it is one of my most powerful guiding principles in life: Risk versus Reward. It is one of the best fucking filters you can introduce into your life. The best thing is, it's simple to use!

It goes a little something like this:

- 💲 When you are faced with a problem or an opportunity, ask yourself: *What's the worst that can happen?* This is your Risk.

- 💲 With the Risk defined, ask yourself *can I handle that outcome?* Because life is all about balance, you have to counteract that with: *What is the best possible outcome if I proceed?*
  You now have a clear Reward.

- 💲 If the answer is "Yes!" go ahead! If it answer is "No," it is not the right opportunity, or you haven't quite nailed the solution to your problem.

So let's revisit your earlier answers in your journal. Run them through the Risk versus Reward filter.

- 💲 What is the Risk of continuing to make myself small?

- 💲 How awesome would the Reward be if I stepped into my power and set myself free from worry and fear?

CHAPTER 4
FAMILY

"Dreams can come true
Look at me babe, I'm with you
You know you gotta have hope
You know you gotta be strong."

I took so much strength from Gabrielle's 1993 hit song "Dreams." It was on repeat on my iPod playlist as I caught the tube into work each day. Even now when I hear any part of that song, I remember sitting on the bench in the middle of London, having undergone the first part of the transformation that cemented who I am today.

After living a whole new life in London for thirty months, I knew I had achieved what I needed to achieve. I'd seen so many European countries, worked for Robert Walters and clocked up more credibility for my career, experienced life as a young single woman with no strings, and learned a shitload about myself through it all.

I was ready to come back to Australia and see my friends and family. At the age of twenty-seven, I was ready to start again from a more solid position. I had learned how to be on my own, how to survive heartbreak, and how to work through those tough nights when you are half a world away from the people who know you the best. I doubled down on my resilience.

My mindset had shifted greatly. I was confident I could go after anything I wanted and be free to be louder than ever, because I no longer felt like I needed to suppress myself. I was always driven, but now, I was proudly independent and fierce because I trusted myself.

When I returned to Australia in 2009, I had a new-found outlook on life; I was never again going to make myself small for someone else... ever!

> I had tried for so long to get a seat on other people's wagons, because when I was with someone else, I felt safe. But then I got my own bloody wagon.

There are always seats on my wagon for anyone who wants to come along for the ride with me, but I will not steer off course if you need to make a detour along the way. Have you reached the stage where you were prepared to captain your own ship?

Being single and career-focused, there was nothing tying me to the Sunshine Coast, so when an opportunity came up for a major recruitment company in Biloela, Central Queensland, I jumped at it. I started as a business development manager before quickly moving into upper management, where I managed a major coal company account with up to 450 contractors and five staff members at one time. There was something about being out on site with steel caps and high-vis on that was right up my alley. The role showed me a lot about what it takes to run a business, and keeping tabs on so many contractors had me feeling as happy as a pig in shit.

From there, I left for a job in Mackay to head up a recruitment division with a team of ten and payroll temps of around 120. When I arrived, it was ranked seventh in the country, and I built it up to sit at number one. My time in Mackay was life-changing in more ways than one. It was in July 2012 that I nearly died in my skydiving accident, and just two months later, I met the love of my life... Jay Langford.

When I was released from hospital following surgery on my broken ankle, I had several plates and screws in me, and those bloody things have made it fun to go through airport security for the rest of my life! I asked my sister to take me to the headquarters of the skydiving business, as I was rightly pissed off by what had happened. I knew it was one of those things they couldn't really control, but I just wanted my money back because of the bad experience. I was in a wheelchair, so my sister wheeled me in so I could talk with the manager. They wouldn't even entertain the idea of a refund, which only riled me up even further! I realised later it was because it would open them up to liability by admitting fault for the accident.

Feeling angry as hell that I'd been denied a simple refund for almost dying, my sister drove me from Cairns to my parents' place on the Sunshine Coast so they could take care of me while I recovered from surgery.

The nineteen-hour drive was horrendous. I was in the back seat on 20 mg of oxycodone, and I was delirious and still in pain. I returned back to Mackay several weeks later with a moon boot but felt physically much stronger and ready for action once more.

My time away from work gave me the opportunity to look at my personal life. I was ready to start looking for a serious relationship and created a profile on the Plenty of Fish dating site. I had been dating on and off for two years before I saw the profile of a man named Jay Langford. I had met a lot of not-so-great guys through the site, but I knew what I wanted and was not prepared to settle for anything less. If I got even a hint of arrogance or condescension on a date, those douchebags were blacklisted, and I never spoke to them again. Life is too short to waste on people who I'm not vibing with, and I certainly didn't want a mismatch as a husband!

I didn't have a thorough checklist, but I knew I didn't need money or a career-driven person. All I wanted was a man with a solid heart who would be a supportive husband and connected father. My first impressions of Jay after reading his Plenty of Fish profile were incredible! He looked cute, had a lot of similar interests to me, and seemed like he had a balance of masculinity and gentleness. Being the strong woman I am, I reached out to connect with him.

We had a couple of chats over messages before I got sick of writing and just wanted to meet him. It was 7 September 2012 when we arranged to meet at the Andergrove Tavern in Mackay. I rocked up in my moon boot, which restricted my outfit choice a little, but Jay didn't seem to mind. We couldn't stop talking as we ate and had a couple of drinks. When I found out his mother's name was Dianne, I decided to sing a song to her on a karaoke mic. I guess maybe I'd had more than a couple of drinks by that stage?

Anyway, Jay and I started dating from there. I was a branch manager at the time, which kept my days full, but I caught up with Jay as often as I could in the evenings. After seven weeks, things didn't seem to be progressing. I felt like I was getting the run-around from Jay, and I wasn't standing for it. I was thirty, and I knew what I wanted. I was on the hunt for someone who would be a great husband and a hands-on father – and I knew Jay fit the bill, so I called him and laid it all out.

"Look, mate, are you in, or are you out? I know that I like you; I don't know what you want, so I need you to tell me, are you keen?"

He didn't give much away over the phone, but he invited me to his place for dinner that night. I arrived to the distinct smell of tuna and realised that he'd made me tuna bake. I absolutely *hate* tuna. But I sat there and tried my best to eat it without cringing too much every time the fork came up to my mouth. God, tuna is bloody awful! It was the first and last meal he ever made for me.

After dinner, he presented me with a white flower and said, "Yes, Kate, I'm all in."

Things progressed quickly from there. Jay had to move out of his place, and we decided to try living together. Three months later, I had fallen for Jay and told him I loved him. He replied with, "Thanks." I felt like he'd just sucker-punched me to the gut. It wasn't until later that I realised that he just needed more time, because Jay is not very open with his emotions. I have the ability to see people's core, and I knew that Jay was vulnerable and connected to me, even if he couldn't see it himself for a while. When Jay first told me he loved me, it meant so much more because of that.

Jay has been a constant in my life ever since. A solid foundation. When I go to bed at night, he makes sure there is a glass of water on my bedside table. He makes me feel safe and accepted for the crazy person that I am. He does everything he can to help me get through my to-do list every single day. No matter what goes on for me during the day, if we are okay, then I can take on anything.

Although I hadn't yet learned the word, I could feel that I was slipping into a *così così* life. I knew there was something more; I could feel it in my bones. In 2013, I started my own résumé-writing business as a side hustle. I realised I had some entrepreneurship skills, and I wanted to explore them. I dipped my toe in by launching Above and Beyond Resumes. I loved having the opportunity to help people one-on-one and to give them guidance on how to apply for the job of their dreams. Hearing their wins lit me up in a completely different way compared to gaining wins for my employers.

I knew I was ready to settle down, and we decided to try for a baby. Jay had shown me he had true integrity, strong morals, and family values. Although he was earning good money working in the mines, he was not driven by money. To him, it was more important how you treat people and what you stand for. He loved the outdoors and spending time with me. Jay ticked all of the boxes, and I couldn't wait to start a family with him.

> There has always been an undercurrent in my world that starting a family would mean that I would have to step back from my career to focus solely on raising my children.

Jay and I were so fortunate that I fell pregnant the first time we tried. We made the decision to move back to the Sunshine Coast to raise our family. I had my immediate family and twenty cousins on the Coast, so I always knew I would end up back there when I became a mother. I wanted my kids to have the same beachside, outdoor lifestyle I had loved when I was growing up.

Leroy was born in Nambour Hospital on 29 June 2014, close to thirty-one years after I had arrived in the same maternity suite. I was on cloud nine that I had a healthy baby boy, a loving partner (who still hadn't pulled his finger out and proposed), a wonderful home on the Sunshine Coast, and flexibility in my work. I thought I would be a younger mum, to be honest, but everything else was just as I had pictured it in my big life plan.

Leroy was two weeks late, and I had to go through an emergency caesarean as he was ten pounds and one ounce – a plump 4.56 kilogram cherub. It broke my heart that I never got to have that first skin-to-skin cuddle that all of the midwives were raving about when we were preparing for labour. In fact, I didn't get it with any of my three children; Gracie was premature and was whisked into the special care unit, and Lincoln also arrived by C-section and was taken away to be assessed as soon as he was out. It is something I'm still emotional about, even though they have all given me millions of cuddles since.

I was pregnant again in early 2015, and I had picked up Above and Beyond Resumes, as it was something I could do while caring for Leroy. Yes, you read that right!

 You can absolutely build your work around children.

There was no way I was going to let motherhood stop me from doing things I was passionate about, and my side-hustle business was something I absolutely loved.

My daughter Gracie was a premature bub born on 23 December. She was supposed to come out on Valentine's Day 2016, but she decided to arrive at thirty-two weeks. Her early arrival was no surprise, as my second pregnancy was very different to my first. I started bleeding at fifteen weeks, and doctors went through several different possible causes but could never work out why it was happening. It just would not stop. By twenty-two weeks, which is when a premature baby has a greater chance of survival, I was sent down to Brisbane to be monitored. I stayed there on bed rest from October to December, despite having a one-year-old at home and a husband working full-time.

I felt so alone in that room, only able to see Jay and Leroy once a week. Being away from Leroy was painfully hard, and with little to do other than be with my own thoughts – there's only so much daytime TV you can watch – I would wonder what he was doing and if he missed me. I know I ached to be with him and for Jay to wrap me in his arms so he could tell me everything would be okay. Instead, it was up to me and this little baby inside me to work together to keep her safe.

Being in a bed for two and a half months is no walk in the park! Sure, it sounds easy, but every time I stood up, I'd bleed. I had to endure internal examinations every day. I never questioned the process, because I knew I would do anything it took to keep my baby alive.

When I reached thirty-two weeks gestation, they let me go back to the Sunny Coast, because they could cater for a premature arrival at that stage in the local neonatal ward. I was only home for a few days before I started to have pain. I had lived with a dull ache that went along with the cramping and bleeding since I was fifteen weeks pregnant, but there was an intensity to this pain that felt scary.

It didn't feel anything like the contractions I had experienced when I was in labour with Leroy, so I called the hospital to talk to my doctor. They sent an ambulance over as a precaution, as I was a high-risk case. Halfway to the hospital, the pains gripped my body again, and I gritted my teeth. The moment I was whisked up to the maternity ward, the midwife declared, "You are in labour!" She started preparing everything, and my mind went almost blank. *How is this possible?* I was in complete denial that it was actually happening. *It's too early. I've only just got out of hospital!*

After having a caesarean with Leroy, I had wanted to have a natural birth, but when the baby's heart rate dropped, I was sped into surgery and prepped. Once I got there, I was ten centimetres dilated, and the surgeon said the baby looked small enough to be delivered without too much trouble with the use of forceps. I agreed, and the moment she was born, she was whisked off to special care.

Gracie was three pounds, just 1.6 kilograms, almost a third of the size her older brother had been. She spent the first eight weeks of her life in Nambour Hospital. I sat by her humidicrib every day, pumping breast milk and feeding her through the neotube. I couldn't hold her in my arms until she was a week old. It was so hard for her to be so close, yet so far. All I wanted to do was wrap her in my arms and never let her go. My little warrior. From the moment I was allowed to hold her, we had skin-to-skin for as long as I possibly could each day so we could begin to build that bond.

I pledge to start a charity that will allow me to gift payments to parents with unexpected premature babies in the ICU wards so they can stay in hospital with their newborns with less financial stress. I know how much emotional and physical stress mothers are under in those situations, and one of the strongest sources of comfort for me was having Jay there. I want to be able to gift other families the opportunity to be together during those times without having the stress of the father having to leave to go back to work.

Gracie came home late January 2016.

After being away from Leroy for such a critical part of his life, and having so much disconnect from Gracie in her first weeks of life, I was so happy to have the four of us at home. Leroy adores his sister, and they have grown into proper siblings with a love/hate relationship. They look out for one another and nurture each other so much that it's ridiculous, but there are times when they will butt heads.

Gracie is strong – she had to be just to make it into this world. I found out after they sent away my placenta that it had been infected, and it was half dead. That was what was causing all of the bleeding. If her middle name wasn't Kate (an ode to the amount of time we spent together in hospital), then it would be Resilience. Gracie can definitely hold her own in most situations, but her kryptonite is her father. Whenever she is around Jay, she transforms into a daddy's girl and gets sooky.

I took twelve months off after having Gracie to be a stay-at-home mum. I loved that time with my babies and would never trade it for anything. You can see how our definition of "having it all" can change. When I was a stay-at-home mum, I felt grateful to be supported by Jay so I could bond with our children and give them the strongest foundation in life. At the time, that was having it all for me.

But after a year, I was ready to go back to work, because the intellectual part of my brain was just crying out for a challenge.

> My definition of having it all then shifted towards being present for my babies but also teaching them resilience by going to kindy and day care so I could stimulate my mind.

I found an opportunity in HR assisting businesses to hire and onboard their teams. I then moved on to another business, where I was tasked with opening a Darwin branch. I enjoyed the balance of being a mum and working two days a week for an employer. I also spent a day a week working in Above and Beyond Resumes and the rest of my time was dedicated to my children. There was a shift that happened for me, and I think this happens for most mothers; something is unearthed that really makes you focus on your "why" and the big picture. Do you know what I mean? My whole world perspective changed, because life was no longer about just about me and Jay; there were actual humans we had to keep alive and nurture well so they would become decent humans.

Jay took his time to ask me to marry him. I'm impatient at the best of times and was getting slightly irritated. We had been together for four years and had two children before he proposed. We were on a family holiday at the Gold Coast, and Jay had picked his time and place. We'd had a busy day, and I walked out of our unit with two screaming kids and a towel wrapped around me from having a shower and found Jay on one knee with rose petals on the floor, a bunch of roses, and champagne on ice.

Jay wishes he could have done it differently, but it was a true snapshot of what our family life was like at the time, screaming kids and all. Despite the hilarity of the moment, I said, "Yes," and we were married a year later.

Gold Nuggets for Family

Family to me is my husband and three children, but I acknowledge that family can have different definitions for every person. It might be a partner. It might be only your children. It might be your fur babies. However you define family, own it!

I don't even remember how many people told me I would sacrifice my successful recruitment career when I decided to have my babies. Or the others who told me I could never run a business if I was a mum. Ha! I bloody showed them! And you can, too!

It is no secret that family is my "why," so I have four categories that I am big on maintaining in our family unit.

Unconditional Love

Even if we do something wrong as humans, we still love each other unconditionally.

Even if we argue, we still love each other. It is the foundation of a strong family unit.

- ⓢ What behaviour can *you* change to model unconditional love?

- ⓢ How can you build an environment of acceptance in your family?

- ⓢ What ways connect more with your family?

Rules

Boundaries are important in any family, as they outline what we expect of each other.

- (💲) What are the top three non-negotiable rules in your family?
- (💲) How do you reward those who respect the boundaries?
- (💲) How do you reprimand those who step out of the boundaries?

Discipline

Routine is essential to having it all! Without it, life is a hot mess! But this is something the family needs to be on board with or it will never work.

- (💲) Is everyone clear on the weekday and weekend routines?
- (💲) When is your connection time?
- (💲) How does everyone pitch in to get everything done?

Fun

Having fun in everything you do makes life more enjoyable and also creates memories you will cherish forever.

- (💲) What is your connection time?
- (💲) What family "traditions" can you create? (For example, we go around the dinner table every night and say what we are grateful for)
- (💲) When can you build in time to be silly?

CHAPTER 5
BUSINESS

When the flower delivery guy walked through the office and stopped at my desk, I'd hear, "Is Kate getting flowers again?" *Hell yes, I am! Because I'm changing their lives!* Knowing that the people I helped noticed how I was going above and beyond in the recruitment world was all the validation I needed.

I knew I had what it took to connect with clients; the fact I received thank you gifts and flowers regularly was a giveaway that I was making real change in their lives.

I had seen a gap in the recruitment industry for a while, but I was too afraid to step up and do it myself. There were always excuses: *I don't have the money. I've got two young children. I don't have the time. I don't know how to run a business...* The list went on and on. I was frustrated as hell with myself, because every time I thought I could take a chance, the excuses would cycle on repeat once more.

I had stayed in a part-time role for about eighteen months before I realised that I had strayed into a *cosi cosi* life. It happens so easily, you know. I was happy, I was making good money, I knew what I was doing. Sounds effortless, right? Like a dream life. It may be for some, but it was grinding me down, because I wasn't *fulfilled*. I had restarted Above and Beyond Resumes and looked at how I could expand it out. When I spoke to people about feeling stuck, they immediately suggested that I start my own recruitment agency, but there was no spark of passion there for me. The internal voice that I use as my compass in life was screaming *NO!*

> *Life is not just about doing what you know; it's about doing what you love.*

I could do résumés. I could do recruitment. Did I want to do either of them in a full-time business? No. Although things had been ticking along with Above and Beyond Resumes, I was faced with the ultimate crossroads; do I start something brand new for myself? Or do I stick with what I know? The latter was the easy option, because it was safe. But I was ready to shake things up!

In January 2018, I started Kate Langford Career Consulting (KLCC). I was conflicted about using my name because it felt egotistical – like I was putting my name up in lights because I was up myself. But when I spoke with people I trusted, they told me my name was actually the major drawcard for my business. It was what made me stand out in the industry, because there was only one of me. It also spoke to my credibility, because my name had been a constant companion (funny how that works…), and it had shown up around the world in the recruitment industry, so people would feel safe knowing I knew my stuff. Once I heard that advice, there was no way I was going to settle for something generic and hide behind a fancy name. I was going to own it!

Was I a certified career consultant? No, but I never let that stop me. By that stage, I had diplomas in counselling, human resources, and management, as well as fifteen years of experience in interacting with employees and employers. I get so frustrated by the number of people who tell me they can't do something because they don't have the piece of paper to say that they can. It can be a confidence-blocker for so many, but that's not going to be you!

Most of the time, your lived experience and professional knowledge are the only tools you need to do something successfully. The only time I would tell someone they *needed* a degree or other qualification was if it is a regulated industry or if they needed to undertake years of training to have the skills they would need, like if they wanted to become a doctor or lawyer. The rest of the time, you will undoubtedly have transferrable skills you can move into your next job opportunity or business.

I have never been an academic; remember, I was the girl who graduated high school with an OP that was very middle of the road. Am I embarrassed by that? No! I may have been an average student, but I found emotional intelligence got me further. My dad's saying, "Whatever you do, be the best at it," was ingrained in me. I knew if I was a garbage collector, I'd be the best fucking garbage collector in Australia, if not the world. That level was what I aspired to. Neither of my parents pushed me towards university study, but I gave a Bachelor of Social Work a go at Queensland University of Technology in Carseldine. I lived and studied in Brisbane for six months before I realised it was not where I wanted to be. I didn't feel like I could truly learn how to help someone by writing assessment pieces; I wanted to actually be out there helping them!

I now have a graduate certificate in career development and am a member of the Career Industry Council of Australia (CICA) because I am extremely passionate about what I do and wanted to achieve the highest level of credibility in that field so clients know I meet professional standards. *Whatever you do, be the best at it.* Back in 2018, I absolutely could have let that lack of qualification stop me. It has stopped so many people that it would break my heart to know the number.

As it turned out, it wasn't a lack of belief in myself or a lack of a piece of paper that would be my first major hurdle in business...

I created a basic website for KLCC to anchor my résumé-writing services and to also add career consulting for the first time. Résumé writing was the bread and butter, but I loved how it evolved as more people came on board with assistance with LinkedIn profiles, addressing selection criteria, and interview coaching so they could put their best foot forward as they advanced through the employment process.

Everything was going smoothly for several months until, one afternoon, I was summoned into my employer's office. My boss opened up a laptop and pointed to my website, telling me that I needed to go home immediately, because it had just come to their attention, and they needed to investigate what was going on. I felt intimidated and upset because I had done nothing wrong. The business I worked for did nothing along the lines of career consulting, and that's why there was a gap to fill.

I packed up and went home, completely distraught. I felt like I was being treated like a criminal who had the sole intention of destroying the business I was employed by. I went back in the next day and was given an ultimatum; leave my job or close my website down. They cited KLCC as being a conflict of interest.

I will never know why they reacted the way they did when I had done nothing but give my all to help them build their business. I was making them tens of thousands each month, and this put me in such a tough spot. I wanted to leave on principle. I wanted to quit so I could go and build my own successful business. But... I had a family to consider and knew an emotional decision to quit would not serve anyone.

I decided to pull down the website and stay.

Not what you expected to read, was it?

As a critical thinker, I will always think, *What is the risk versus the reward?* If the scales are tipped too far to the risk side, I will likely park the idea. At that time, the money was tipping the scales in favour of me not pursing my business. I needed to be able to provide for my family, and so it was too risky to leave my steady, reliable job to take a punt.

I didn't have a lot of savings to fall back on that would allow me to be comfortable to take the risk and know that Jay and I could still cover all of our expenses as a household. I have always taken my responsibility as a parent seriously and never wanted to put my family in a tight financial situation just so I could blindly follow my dreams.

Let me tell you, the decision was the safe one, but I felt saddened by it all. Dad could see that the situation was eating me up. I had to keep showing up for my employers and my clients, even though my heart was no longer truly in it anymore.

Dad has always been my number one fan, and when he learned that money was the only thing tipping the scales away from me pursuing my business, he stepped in. He called me up while I was at work and began a conversation that changed my life.

"So Kate, what's it going to take for you to do this?"

"Do what, Dad?"

"Start your own business."

"I dunno, Dad. I've got two little kids under three and two mortgages..."

"Well, what if I pay you $500 a week until you get on your feet?"

"Are you serious?" I got up out of my chair and walked out of the office. "You can't do that, Dad."

"Nope! I'm doin' it, Kate. I'm going to pay you $500 a week so you can get out of there."

"Oh my God..."

"I believe in you, Kate. I know you can do this."

You'd think I'd jump for joy, right? But the part of me that prided myself on being independent and self-sufficient was deeply challenged at that moment. I bawled my eyes out when we got off the phone. I had never said yes to an offer like that in my entire life. I had paid for my first car at seventeen with the money I'd saved up for three years. I had paid for all of my travels. I had bought my first home on my own. I prided myself on being independent.

If I accept this, I don't have anything standing in my way... I can go all in. I am out of excuses...

There were two more questions I had to ask myself, and this ran through my head at lightning speed while Dad was still on the other end of the line: *What is the worst case scenario here?*

Well, the worst case is I don't get enough clients on board to sustain the business, and I have to get a job. Dad has offered me this money without any strings, so there is no financial risk. The worst case if I don't do this is that I'll never be able to break free from this feeling that there is something much bigger waiting just around the corner for me. I don't want to be old and regret not taking this chance.

The second question: *Can I handle this?*

YES!

"Okay, Dad, thank you, that would be great!"

After that, there was no hesitation. I backed myself and knew I could do it – that was never in question – but now that my financial obligations to my family were taken care of, there was no going back. I was ready to jump in with both feet and resigned the next day.

On 26 April 2018, KLCC became my full-time gig.

I knew I needed to create a fresh new space that would reflect my huge vision for KLCC, and the little nook where I'd spent hours writing résumés for Above and Beyond just wasn't going to cut it. Jay and I talked about it, and I'd always wanted to create a fourth bedroom for a future third child, so we transformed the garage into two rooms. I was pleased that I'd managed to not only create an energetic new space for KLCC, but it would also serve to help me manifest my third baby – multitasking at its finest!

When looking through the colour swatches, I felt drawn to the vibrancy for raspberry red. I marvelled at how empowered the deep raspberry red made me feel. *Yes, this will do perfectly!* A firm believer in energy, I knew that empowering and uplifting energy would flow through to my clients with me as the conduit.

I bought a tin and splashed a few licks of paint on the walls of my new office and put several whiteboards in there ready to go. I love a good whiteboard! There is something about being able to jot down all of my thoughts to clear my mind and then be able to wipe it clean and start again that gets me excited. There is always something new, something more, something outside of the box, and I can capture them instantly on my whiteboards.

While I was steady in my ability and commitment to making KLCC a success, not everyone in my world was supportive. I was hearing all kinds of things:

"You can't have a business with such small children! Who will look after them?"

"Why aren't you staying in recruitment?"

"It's a competitive market, Kate. How are you going to compete?"

"Why don't you wait until the kids are older?"

"How will you find the time?"

The naysayers made me even more determined to prove that I *could* have it all. That I could run a highly successful business, be an engaged and present mother, have time with my husband, and still look after my mental and physical well-being. I was so sick of people asking me how I planned to do it – all I knew was I *could* bloody do this!

In fact, I knew that running my own business was the only way I *could* have it all. There are many people who are not designed to be bosses. They are the perfect employees and can have great success and feel fulfilled by moving up the ranks in someone else's business. But that wasn't me. I didn't fit the mould. I didn't like being confined. I didn't feel like I was alive unless I was creating, and it's hard to create when you are restricted by someone else's framework. By that stage, I hadn't found a boss who would allow me to truly fly, so I had to spread my own wings and run headfirst towards that cliff to take the leap.

Be careful, though, because not everyone is cut out to be a boss themselves.

> What I've found is that people who want to start their own businesses generally fall into one of two camps: they are either running from something, or they have a burning desire to do something.

If you want to create something and are passionate about it, you have a reason to serve, and the creation becomes bigger than you. In that zone, you are in flow, and time becomes your friend. However, if you are running from something, you will be less inclined to get into the trenches and do what it takes to build something from nothing. If you are running from something, you are not a business owner. That's a cold, hard fact that I have had to share with so many people who have come to me for career coaching and have been toying with the idea of branching out on their own.

I believe a lot of business owners are actually running from something – I would say fifty-nine out of every sixty. That's my stat, by the way, but when you consider that it has been widely reported that sixty percent of small businesses fail within their first three years, you can see how I believe only one in sixty people start a business they are passionate about.

When you consider small and medium-sized businesses make up ninety-eight percent of all business in Australia, that's a scary large failure rate. People who want to start their own business out of passion are wired differently. They are often the odd ones out. They don't see the world the way other people do. They crave opportunity and strive for success and achievement within themselves. They butt heads with managers and employers, and their ideas are often shut down because they are outside the square. If you are that person, when you find entrepreneurship, you will feel like you are home.

In my experience, those who are running from something end up being "gonnas": "I'm gonna make a phone call," "I'm gonna build a website..." on and on it goes. Everything they need to do, they are *going* to do. Why? Because the passion isn't there. I often can sniff out a "gonna," because they tell me they want to start a business because it gives them flexibility. If that's the first reason they give me, I shut them down, because they are going into business for the wrong reasons.

I get frustrated to no end by "gonnas." True business owners are "doers." They see something that needs to be done, and they just fucking do it. Sorry, not sorry. There is a method to creating a successful, sustainable business and you will never find a "gonna" at the head of one.

There was no time to celebrate this huge life change. I just rolled up my sleeves and got to work. Dad's offer gave me permission to start something I had been thinking about for a long time, so I was just ready to start helping people as fast as possible. I was excited to get to my desk in my shiny new raspberry-red office and change lives.

Gold nuggets for business

I run whole courses and coaching programs around this topic, so these are the top tips I can give to you for now. If you want to do a deep dive and throw yourself right in, reach out, and let's make some magic! Believe me when I say that friends and family are sometimes the *worst* people to talk to about your business idea. They will either become your unwavering cheerleader even if your idea is shit, or they will be busy telling you it's a shit idea to take a risk even if your idea is incredible!

There are four hard questions you need to stop right now and ask yourself if you are thinking of starting a business rather than seeking a more rewarding career:

1. Are you a business owner?
Not everyone is cut out for business. If you want to have more time with your kids, you can create a career around that; it's not enough of a reason to take the risk of starting a business. There is a shit ton of work that goes into building a business, and more often than not, you are responsible for *all* of it. Likewise, if you are driven by money, you will find it hard to weather the start-up phase where it is very rare to see the zeros stacking up in the bank account.

If you are sick and tired of your career or have a shit boss and are looking for an escape, you are not automatically going to be a good business owner, because you are running from that situation and using a business as an escape. That's really not great energy to bring into something you are building; it breeds negativity and desperation, because you want it to work so bad so you don't have to go back.

A true business owner is driven by passion. They have found a way to serve and make a difference through a product or service.

So take some time to truly think about where you lie on this spectrum.

- ⓢ Are you passionate about your idea?

- ⓢ Is it something you have thrown together to get you out of another situation?

- ⓢ Are you in the middle? Your idea may only need a few tweaks to become something you are prepared to throw one hundred percent of yourself behind.

2. What do you want to do with your business?

- ⓢ Are you planning to be a solopreneur, or do you want to build an empire? There is no right or wrong here, but you need to be clear, because these two directions are polar opposites and require very different foundations to be built at the start.

- ⓢ What is your "why?"

3. How are you different?

Without falling into the rabbit hole of despair that is comparison, undertake a very brief period of market research to see who your competitors are.

- ⓢ Can you find a niche that makes you different?
- ⓢ What is your point of credibility?
- ⓢ Do you have tenure and decades of experience on the board?
- ⓢ Do you have degrees or other professional qualifications? (Don't let this be a dream-killer if you don't! Just remember my story!)

4. Who are you serving?

Know your target market. If you don't know your niche and target market, then you're going to be like everyone else, and you will never be able to cut through the noise. Remember, I started out wanting to help back-to-work mums, but when I investigated what that would look like, I realised one of their pain points was that they could not afford the services I wanted to offer to them; it was a chicken and egg situation! They needed the services to get a job they wanted, but because they had not worked for a while, they had no disposable income to pay for them.

- ⓢ Rather than assuming what your market wants, roll your sleeves up and ask them!
- ⓢ What are your clients struggling with?

- 💲 What are their pain points?
- 💲 What do they really hate that you can take off their hands?
- 💲 Better still, how will they feel once that have the outcome they are looking for?

Not only will you get an understanding of who needs you the most and how you can best serve them, but you will also learn the language they use, and this will be invaluable when the time comes to start connecting with your target market to bring in clients.

CHAPTER 6
TIME

If you think there is not enough time to follow your dreams, you just don't want them badly enough. I was thirty-five years old and had a three- and four-year-old tearing around home when I started KLCC. There were plenty of people who told me I was crazy and that I would never have enough hours in the day to get everything done. But guess what? I made time.

If you think you don't have time to do something, you are barking up the wrong tree.

> When you are passionate about something, time is not an issue.

If it is, you just don't want to do it, or you can't be bothered, or you're procrastinating, or it's not a genius zone, or it's boring, or it's not lighting you up.

Even when I had Above and Beyond Resumes and was also working part-time as an employee with two children under three, I would find time to do it all! When everyone else was asleep, I'd go to my desk and stay up until eleven o'clock at night working on résumés, because I just couldn't get enough of it! I was so excited by getting results for my clients and helping them to land their dream job that I would be full of adrenaline as I created their résumés for them. I was like an addict and couldn't *not* do it.

It's like the feeling you get when you pick up a good book and you can't put it down because it's a real page-turner. You might not think you have the time to dedicate to reading an entire book, but once you are swept away by the words, you become passionate about finding out what happens, and time is no longer a relevant thing.

It grinds me when people say they don't have time for something they claim to be passionate about. I have found that there is *always* time for whatever lights you up. I believe when true entrepreneurs find their business, it feels like home. It was instant for me. From the moment I sat behind my desk as the CEO of KLCC, I felt like I could fly, think, achieve, motivate, pump others up. There was a sense of excitement about what was next and how I could bring my vision to life. I never doubted it. Never.

That's why I had to wait for that final piece of the puzzle to land for me to find my direction in career consulting. There is a reason why I didn't start years earlier and build a business around recruitment – it wasn't my passion.

While my clients are important, my kids are my purpose for being a successful businesswoman. If I am the best at what I do, I can build a team, and that frees me up to spend more time with them.

I didn't start out working school hours four days a week. Hell no!

Just a few weeks after launching KLCC, I had fifteen résumés on the go and was working career coaching around that. I had started working Monday to Friday and also pulled some nights once the kids went to bed.

I knew there were so many people I could serve, and their lives could be changed once they had the confidence to follow the career path of their dreams. That, coupled with seeing people get results over and over again, helped me gain the momentum and confidence to keep pushing on.

Without it, it's so easy to stop in your tracks. I can't stop, and I won't, because it's not about me; it's about every single person who comes in for help.

> ❝ As soon as you take yourself out of the equation, it propels your business forward, because your energy is all about serving. ❞

I was on a roll and loving every moment of it, and when I came up for air five months later, a harsh realisation slapped me in the face – my time with my family was being compromised. There were so many résumés on my desk that I was burned out. I became irritated whenever I realised the next thing on my list of tasks for the day was to write another résumés. This was the complete opposite to how I used to feel when I was burning the midnight oil writing résumés because I was so excited about handing them to my clients.

There was a vicious cycle that started then; I procrastinated with the writing, because I started to hate it; this meant the résumés spent longer on my desk then they used to, clogging up my pipeline and therefore costing me money, as I couldn't take anything else on.

As an expert in recruiting, this is when I would advise my clients to start to hire people to support them. Now that this person was me, I was shit-scared of doing it. I didn't know if I could sustain a wage for them when I was barely paying myself anything, as it was all being poured back into the business. I didn't know if I could trust someone with my precious clients. It was my first glimpse into being "on the other side," and it was terrifying!

I had to psych myself up and give myself a stern talking-to, just as I had done many times in the past with businesses who needed staff. *You need to do this in order to grow. You are only one person, Kate, and you can only do so much. What is the worst that can happen? You* get someone on board, and money runs out, so you let them go. Can you handle that? It would be disappointing, but the world isn't going to explode if that happens... Yes, I can handle that.

Alright then, just get on with it!

I hired my first part-time personal assistant (PA) in September 2018 to help me lighten the load. This is where time evolves for a businessowner who has been established for a while. As the business grew and more clients came on board, I knew I had to build my workforce so I could start to delegate. Whenever I found myself procrastinating on something, I knew it was time to find someone who would be passionate about that thing I no longer enjoyed.

I am massive on noticing procrastination. If I procrastinate on something, there is a problem. I hold myself just as accountable for it as I do my clients. When you boil it down, it's wasted time and money. Although I am self-aware, there have been times when my team have pulled me up for procrastinating on something. What are the giveaways? I'll go to the toilet just because it means I can go for a walk. I'll stroll out of my office and start conversations with my team about nothing in particular. I'll heat up lunch early. I'll even get out the vacuum cleaner and start to give the office a once-over. Usually, by the time the vacuum comes out, the team are onto me.

"Kate, what are you doing?"

"Well, I'm just vacuuming. I saw some crumbs under my desk and figured I'd just clean the whole room while I'm at it."

"Right, so what were you avoiding?"

"Well, I have to write notes for a presentation…"

"So why are you vacuuming when you have a presentation to write?"

"Hmmmmm… Shit. I don't want to write it."

Boom!

Of course, there was a reason why I was vacuuming, and it had absolutely nothing to do with crumbs! Usually, I would delegate an activity I procrastinate on to one of my team, but as I was the one giving the presentation, I needed to craft notes that I would be able to work with and understand. It wasn't something I could handball. I'm grateful when people call me out on my BS, and that's why I readily do it for others. So what did I do? I put the vacuum away, put my big girl pants on, and ate the damn frog (do the difficult thing first).

The great thing was, once that presentation was written, I powered on through the PowerPoint creation and even added effects and fading in and out. *Urgh.* But then I could rinse and repeat it as many times as I needed to in the future. I'm a believer in doing something right the first time, and then it's done. As much as I am a doer, I am also human, so I need people around me who can call me out and hold up that mirror when I need it.

It is so much easier to stay in flow and manage your time well when you stay in your genius zone. I learned to delegate very quickly because efficiency is king. PowerPoint and graphic design, for instance, are not my genius zone. I suck at both of them. Anything creative that needs attention to small details is not me; I operate with big-picture thinking and anything systematic. It would take me a couple of hours to pull together a small design for our social media, for example, when someone on my team could do it in less than half an hour. Time is money.

> Whenever you are not in your genius zone, you literally watch money pouring out of your business.

As résumé writing was at the top of my procrastination-inducing list, I started to outsource the résumé writing as well. I taught my PA everything I did, and she quickly grasped how I wanted things done. It felt so liberating to be able to have someone working alongside me. My PA became the main coordinator for the résumé writers, which I had based offshore to start with in order to keep my costs down. As soon as I could afford to, I brought that work back into Australia and have had Aussie writers working for me ever since.

Whenever I feel myself burning out with stuff I don't like, I take notice. I know I would never take that service away, because it is something people need and value, so the answer is to get someone else on board to do it. Although it felt like a financial stretch at the time, being able to outsource by reinvesting my small profit freed me up to gain momentum. I know this can be a *huge* barrier for some people, but if you can take a temporary financial hit for a minute and still cover your bills, you've got to do it.

It comes back to what is important for you. For me, it was three things: serving as many people as I could, freeing up my time so I could spend it with my family, and growing my business.

As you know, my family is my "why," so anything that affects my ability to be present with my husband and kids needs to be addressed pretty quickly, or else I feel like I am busting my arse for no good reason. There was a third reason I wanted to bring on my first employee – it was my first step towards building a large team that could one day take my business global. Ten million turnover in ten years, that was the medium-term goal!

Your goals could be very different. Maybe you just want to be a one-man band. But if you do want to scale, there has to be a sacrifice somewhere in there. By that, I mean meeting your needs before getting your wants! It is a basic economic principle: always cover the boring things like the bills, and whatever is left over is what you can play with. So as long as the needs are met, the wants can come.

Believe me when I say, though, that the wants will never come unless you do the bloody work. This shit doesn't happen by itself!

> ❛ If you want to have your cake and eat it too, there is always going to be a building phase that will take your blood, sweat, and tears. ❜

This is where you mix the ingredients for the sponge cake and pop it into the oven. You have to add consistent heat and energy in order for it to grow and rise. Once it is baked, you can then put the cream on top. When you think of the cake baking as your needs and the cream layer as your wants, you get an understanding of how it does take time and sustainable business practices to get you to the place where you can enjoy your rewards. But you have to just start with the sponge!

Jay has backed me all the way, and when I discussed the short-term hit my business income would take by bringing on my first employee, he trusted me completely. I have always dealt with the finances, so I knew where everything stood, and I constantly communicate that with Jay. Coming back to the risk versus reward, having a family and two mortgages was enough for me to know where that line was, but even to this day, if I have had a bad week in business, I might pay myself a little less so we don't take too much of a hit. A lot of people won't agree with that, but as long as I have all the needs covered, I get my wants.

The first real want I received from my business came three years into KLCC; yes, it takes patience! I gave myself a big treat of a $38,000 caravan that we could use to make memories on family holidays. It felt so amazing to gift that to myself after years of hard slog. I also treat myself to weekends away by myself to recharge. As I was writing this book, I went away to Noosa for a weekend and spent $800 a night to have solitude, room service, movies in bed, and lounges by the pool with five-star restaurant meals.

What is the point of life, business, or working hard if you are not reaping the rewards?

The trick is to make sure that the sponge is set, and then the cream tastes even more delicious.

Even though I have a team of fifteen as I write this book, there are still days when time is a precious commodity. While writing this book, I had a day that illustrated perfectly what I still have to do some days just to make it through. So here it is:

I woke up at 6.30 am to a poopy nappy courtesy of Lincoln (whom you will be introduced to in this book shortly!) Jay had already left, as he heads off for work at 6.15 am, so it was on me to clean Lincoln up. It was a theme day at school, and Gracie and Leroy had to wear certain stuff, so we rummaged through their wardrobes to find something that suited. I made them breakfast to eat and prepared lunches for school and started the usual run-through of morning questions: "Do you have your socks on?" "Are your library books in your bag?" "Have you filled up your water bottle?" You know the ones.

That morning, a team member was sick, so I had to reschedule clarity calls and meetings so I could take them on, even though it was meant to be a day I wasn't going into the office.

Gracie was upset because a friend had cancelled her birthday party, so I arranged for her to sleep over with two other girls on Sunday night so she could still have fun. Then I realised she had another commitment on Saturday that clashed with her cheer concert, so I had to ring up another mum to let her know we would only be able to be there for an hour and clear that with her. Then Gracie was happy.

I then had to arrange care for Lincoln, as I was meant to spend the day with him so I could take him to an appointment that afternoon. After a few phone calls, he was taken care of. I prepared dinner and set it in the slow cooker so it would be ready for Jay and the kids that night. All of this was before 8 am, when I had to drop the kids off to school.

I rocked up at work in my gym gear and ran a handover meeting before rushing to get changed into some decent work clothes and do my makeup so I could interview someone in person. I went through a few clarity calls and left to pick up Lincoln at 11.45 am to drive to Brisbane so he could have a test done at the hospital. We got stuck in traffic on the way home and walked in the door at 5.15 pm. Jay had picked up Leroy and Gracie from school, and I had fifteen minutes to shower and change before I had to go out for my netball breakup dinner. I was late, but I made it, and got home at 9 pm.

So don't tell me you're too fucking busy to make shit happen!

You might think, *If that happened to me, I'd be screwed* (I hear that from Jay a lot). But the reality is, uncertainty is normal, and this can happen at any time. I could sit down and stress out, or I could act and just get shit done. These things have to happen, because what I do is important, and I can't let a slight change of plans through everything off course.

If you say you are busy, I get offended, because I am living proof that busy is not an acceptable excuse. It is fair to say we have busy times, but if you want to do it, you are passionate about it, and it fits your purpose in life, you *make* time to do it.

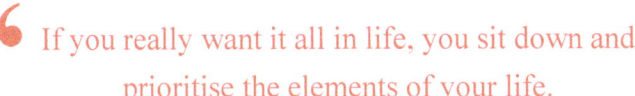

> If you really want it all in life, you sit down and prioritise the elements of your life.

Remember your "why," and structure your life around it. If money was my priority, I would not have stressed about the kids having social calendar clashes and would have just gone to work. But it's not; it never has been. My kids are everything, and being able to take them to appointments, go to swimming carnivals, and play at birthday parties is important to me. I've lost track of the number of times I've rocked up to a school event with a nice work top and jacket on with denim shorts on the bottom. It's like an outfit mullet – business on the top and #mumlife on the bottom!

I cram a *lot* into my days, but I sure as hell make sure I get eight hours of sleep every night. Jay would get up in the night for Lincoln, and I don't carry guilt around that, because that's what I need in order to be a powerhouse during the day.

Gold Nuggets for Time

If you believe you don't have time to do something, you are spending your time doing the wrong things! I know that when you are passionate about something and are driven by goals that support your "why," you will make time to do the things you need to in order to bring them to life.

We all have the same twenty-four hours in a day, yet those who are "doers" will get so much more shit done than those who dawdle through their days. Without focus and passion, you will be a "gonna" and then nothing ever gets done, because you are just kicking the can down the road every day.

I run a busy household with three kids who all have after-school activities and weekend sports to get to. I can still manage to run a million-dollar turnover business with a team of fifteen and spend precious time with my husband most nights. There is still time in my week for me to dedicate space and time to nurture myself and recharge my batteries.

See how doing one thing doesn't mean I can't do something else? You can have it all, and it comes down to simple planning. Get out your journal and write down:

- ⓢ How much time do I want to spend with my kids/partner/fur babies each day?

- ⓢ How much time do I realistically need to achieve my career/business commitments each week?

- ⓢ What is my work overflow limit? (This will become non-negotiable)
- ⓢ How much time do I need to allocate to hobbies, sport, and other activities?
- ⓢ Do I have boundaries in place so I focus on what I am doing without multitasking?
- ⓢ If no, what can I put in place to be more present?

From those results, make yourself a plan! What does each day of the week look like? Remember that shit happens, and this is a plan for an ideal world. You need to have a flexible mindset to know that if something unexpected comes up, one hat may require more presence than another in any given day or even week!

CHAPTER 7
SELF-WORTH

Walking into a luxury home in Adelaide and being met with a dozen ladies, all with perfectly styled hair, stylish designer clothes, full faces of makeup, and American accents was one of the most intimidating things I have done since becoming a businesswoman.

Sometimes, in order to grow into your dream life, you just have to put yourself out there. No matter how scary or uncomfortable it makes you feel, you have to shed all of your defensive mechanisms and wear your vulnerability with pride.

I learned this lesson in early 2019 when I attended my first business retreat. It was run by a woman I had looked up to for years; I'll call her Miss Inspo. Her philosophy of "doing" had not just inspired me but resonated deeply with my own belief system and mindset. Miss Inspo spruiked the power of getting out there and taking action – that constantly doing will get you a lot further than perfection ever will.

I had admired Miss Inspo from afar as she fostered a community of strong, courageous women who had taken the plunge to become leaders of profitable businesses. I craved to be a part of this world. I wanted so badly to get my own business off the ground and to become like these women I had looked up to for so long. I wanted to pick their brains, learn their strategies, and hear their stories.

The people you surround yourself with can make or break your success. Do you feel that? I think I was so attracted to these types of people because, deep down, I knew I had those qualities inside of me too. I wanted to be surrounded by people who would have the power to push me to achieve my own potential.

I had been signed up to Miss Inspo's online business coaching programs and was getting so much out of them. Her teachings were actually the catalyst for my business in a lot of ways. I remember I had been driving around on the Gold Coast for a family holiday when I made the decision to sign up to one of her workshop packages. I was so nervous about it, but I decided I wasn't going to hold back. I had nothing to lose. Adapting the business mindset seemed to come quickly for me. In the very early sessions, they spoke about building a business around what you already know and I thought, *Great!* I knew and had worked in recruiting virtually forever, so I figured that was what I would build my business around.

Initially, I was toying with the idea of building a business coaching service for recruitment agencies so the owners could improve on their approach, because it seemed like the natural progression for me. I also had a desire to help mums get back into the workforce and thought that could be a great niche for me to focus on in what became KLCC. Even from the early stages, I have been passionate about showing women how they can have it all. I wanted to empower mothers so they could pursue the career of their dreams even if they had children at home.

When I started to plan it all out and look at the logistics of it, I quickly realised that I couldn't serve them fully. Although I had the passion for return to work mothers, that market didn't have sustainability, because they couldn't afford the services. It was my first tough lesson in taking the emotion out of business. To ensure KLCC had longevity and could grow and scale, I had to let go of my desire to help just a small section of the community. Obviously, things progressed a little differently, but my business idea came from those very early days of learning everything I could from Miss Inspo online.

Just because I was unable to follow that path right away doesn't mean I have let it go forever. I may revisit it another time, but it is the foundation of my desire to spread the word that women can have their cake and eat it too, and that is why you have this book in your hands! It is still my long-term mission, and the way I do it has evolved over time. From the get-go, KLCC has been helping people to transition in their careers, but now, there is so much mindset education that comes in for career consulting clients that helps to empower them in all areas of life. This has seen women empowered to apply for their dream career even if they have spent decades doing something in a completely different realm of expertise just to pay the bills. They are finding their purpose and passion as employees.

It felt amazing to dive in the pool with the people who signed up for coaching through KLCC and teach them how to transfer their skills to new industries they had always dreamed of working in but didn't think they had the skills for. I was able to openly share my experience of imposter syndrome and how I had transferred all of my skills into coaching. When they realised that you don't have to be a master at something just to give it a go, it connected us on a whole new level, and I got a real kick out of seeing them grow and evolve.

All of this was unfolding without any direct coaching guidance.

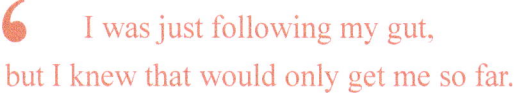

> I was just following my gut,
> but I knew that would only get me so far.

When I saw Miss Inspo was hosting a retreat in the Adelaide in 2019, I just knew I had to find a way to get there. There was one problem, though – at this point in my business, I didn't even have the money to buy a ticket to the event. I thought about letting go of the dream and saving up for the next one, but something inside of me just knew I needed to take a risk and put myself out there. It was a now-or-never moment for me.

I made a phone call to Dad and told him about the retreat. I told him about how much it meant to me and how much I thought I would be able to get out of it. I really believed it was make-or-break for me at the time. As always, Dad was so supportive.

"Kate, if you think this will help you, then do it!"

He told me that if I wanted to have my own business life, then he would do all he could to help me make that a reality. Dad dug deep once more and lent me the five-and-a-half thousand dollars I needed to book myself a spot at the retreat. I was absolutely shitting myself, but I was so excited. I ended the phone call with a promise to pay my dad back, whether the retreat was as revolutionary, as I had played it out to be in my head, or not. I knew in my heart and in my mind that I was going to do that damn thing. There is no way I was going to let my dad down.

One of the main components of the retreat was for participants to get up in front of the hostess and her team of entrepreneurs to pitch their business. It was an open forum for constructive criticism and a starting point for your business model. In the lead up to the retreat, I did all I could to prepare. I practised and practised my pitch, went over my business model, and asked myself a million hypothetical questions just so I would have an answer to anything I could possibly have been asked during the retreat.

When I finally arrived in Adelaide, I was so conflicted. I had never been more excited. I was so full of hope, yet I was filled with all of this self-doubt. I remember standing at the letter box at the top of the driveway of this immaculate property and pacing back and forth. I felt like a total imposter, like I wasn't worthy of being there at all.

Kate, what the hell? You don't belong here with these people! You had to borrow bloody money off your Dad just to buy the ticket! They're going to laugh at you. You are waaaaay out of your league here. It's not too late to turn around and go back home... Save yourself from the embarrassment.

My self-talk was shit. I was in such a spiral. I felt so inferior.

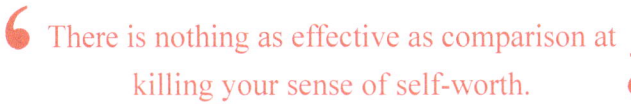

> There is nothing as effective as comparison at killing your sense of self-worth.

Despite all that chatter in my head, bringing me down by the second, there was one strong voice that cut through.

Have you come all this way just to back out, Kate?

"Hell no."

Yes, I answered myself out loud! Luckily, no one was around to witness my moment of madness, but that question was a pivotal moment for me. It smashed all my doubt into smithereens and brought my power back.

In that moment, I could either buckle under the pressure, or I could step up. I could level up in life like I wanted to, or I could stay put. I hadn't travelled all that way and spent all that money to just crumble. I was doing the damn thing. I feel like one of my greatest strengths is finding the courage when I need it. The courage to feel scared and do it anyway. The courage to be vulnerable and resilient.

Vulnerable is probably the best way to describe how I felt throughout the entire retreat. There were twenty participants who had come from all around the world to take part. I felt so intimidated when I met them all. I know this has one thousand percent to do with my perception, because they were all open, warm, and welcoming, but the whole time I was at this retreat, I had to wrestle with my self-worth.

These women I was surrounded by were dressed immaculately, spoke articulately, and were connected with so many prestigious people in business. A lot of the time I felt like little old me – a girl who wasn't very academic and hadn't even paid for her own ticket to the joint! That is what I had to fight through in my mind every day I was there.

A day or so into the retreat, my time finally came to get up in front of the firing squad and pitch my business to these other amazing women. I was so churned up inside. I was literally shaking as I got up from my chair and shuffled over to where I was to stand. I took a deep breath and forged ahead. I let myself be vulnerable and opened up. I think I even started my pitch with something along the lines of, "Well, I don't know if I belong here, but I have this idea, and I have no idea if I'm out of my depth or not…"

Then, I just did my best to pitch the hell out of my idea. I realise now, though, that I wasn't just pitching my business model, I was pitching myself. I was articulating to Miss Inspo and the other women with every single ounce of myself all that I had been through to get to that point.

I remember one of the panel asking me how much money I wanted to be making from my business. I was in the moment and answered honestly by saying, "I just want to make enough money so I can buy healthy food for my family and not have to worry about the bank balance when I go to swipe my card at the checkout." At this point, I was making enough to pay myself a weekly wage of $1,000, but I honestly had no idea if I could sustain that kind of income.

Throughout my pitch, I let my honesty pour out. I wore my heart on my sleeve. I even began to cry at one point when the emotion of it all overwhelmed me. But I persisted and pushed through. I was my true self, and I feel I did not just do my business justice but myself as well. Something happened to me during that pitch; I feel like I was transformed by it in a way. I started accepting that I was creating the life I wanted to live. I was gaining confidence in my own power. I know a lot of people would cringe at getting up and crying in front of a group of influential businesspeople, but I feel like that is what makes me different. I'm me. I'm vulnerable. I'm never hiding behind some kind of mask.

The feedback I received from my pitch was overwhelmingly positive. So many of the women approached me afterwards to congratulate me on how well I had presented. They appreciated the out-of-the-box marketing strategies I had devised. Their validation made me see that I was actually doing some very business savvy things. It cemented to me that the business path was one I was meant to be travelling. I couldn't believe it when I realised other people hadn't thought of doing the same things I was doing organically without anyone guiding me. When influential people I looked up to suddenly wanted a seat saved next to me at the lunch table, I knew I must have been doing something right. And then, when they started pulling out their notebooks and taking notes, well, you could have knocked me over with a feather!

Heck, maybe this business thing is my jam!

 I slowly began to get comfortable inside the uncomfortable. I've come to learn that is the place where growth happens.

This doesn't mean to say I was doing everything perfectly. The pitch was a fantastic opportunity to find the flaws in my business plan and strategies. For a lot of people, having their ideas picked apart by others might just be the thing that makes them crumble. But I was so excited to have finally got my idea out there and to learn from the best about ways I could improve. I tried to soak in as much as I could about business development and marketing strategies. I fired back questions and dug deeper into what other people were doing and why it was working for them.

I took action on the feedback straight away. I was done procrastinating and being stagnant. One of the marketing elements I hadn't yet embraced was the art of the Facebook Live. Pressing record and being streamed around the world to anyone who wanted to watch was something that had terrified me up until that point. *Why would people care what you have to say, Kate? What if you stumble over your words and look like a fool?* My sense of self-worth had shot sky-high as a result of the retreat, and I actually did my very first Live from the house we all stayed at.

I still, to this day, remember doing it, because everyone was watching me. I felt so self-conscious at first, but then I just thought to myself, *Nah, stuff it!* I did it anyway. I have always been someone who likes to take action, to implement things quickly. I think this is because I'm a fast learner, so when I pick up a new skill, I never want to sit on it. I just want to *do*, which is part of the reason I love lists. Add a task, do a task, add a task, do a task, and repeat. I think that is how I have juggled having so many balls in the air at once. I just get in and do.

I would even go as far as saying that you can't have it all unless you become a "doer."

As soon as I came back from the retreat, my business began to change. It sounds cliche, but honestly, it was like it happened overnight. I went from making $5,000 a month to making $30,000 over the next three months. I'd doubled my freaking business!

The wonder lady who had inspired me early in business obviously saw something in me, too. It wasn't long after the retreat that she asked me to come on board to write for and be featured in a book of hers that was being created as part of her online subscription package. She was particularly interested in a marketing strategy I was using to build my business. This was a marketing strategy that ended up going worldwide to her followers. So not only was my income growing, so too was my business persona and name.

The scaling that happened in my business life was phenomenal. More so, the growth that happened for me personally was limitless. I started to feel worthy for the first time in my life. I had gone from this girl who felt like a total imposter to embracing the badass businesswoman inside of me. I stepped up. I fought back against the self-doubt and the shitty self-talk. But it wasn't like I changed into someone I didn't recognise; rather, I found my true self. My authentic self. The self that was born out of vulnerability. I let that woman inside of me flourish. I let her feel worthy. Sure, the business strategies were fantastic, but it was the shift in my mindset that, ultimately, made me successful. And it's kept me successful, too.

> Having it all is seventy percent mindset and thirty percent doing.

I've come to realise the power of vulnerability. I've become the queen of it in my own mind. I am authentic, and I call a spade a spade, which in the business world seems like a rare quality to possess. It has served me well. I've had so many people over the years ask me how I became successful, in business within a short period of time, and the honest-to-god truth is I've just been myself.

These days, I will not work with clients who aren't willing to show their vulnerability. I'm not interested in people's hard outer layer, and quite frankly, I have a bullshit radar the size of a large continent. If you can't show me your true self, bye bye! To me, that just shows that you aren't willing to be coached, and I honestly don't have the time or energy for that. If you can't be vulnerable, then you can't be successful. Full stop.

Gold Nuggets for Self-Worth

There was a time when I would have cringed the moment those words came out of my mouth, but that was just because I didn't recognise my own worth.

I acknowledge the things I do that I think are awesome and celebrate them with myself and the people closest to me. I'm not up myself, though. There's a line between confidence and arrogance – a fine line. People can go too far that way because they lose their humility. Keeping yourself in check is possible when you are humble and know that you will make mistakes. I love making mistakes, because I don't believe in failure; mistakes are learning.

Vulnerability and authenticity have become the two qualities that I seek out more than any other. The people I respect most aren't afraid to show those sides of themselves. Vulnerability is particularly important, because I feel like it shows that you have done the hard yards, you've looked deep enough to recognise your own faults and shortcomings, and you are humble enough to seek improvement. Being vulnerable means you aren't just going to quit the second something doesn't go to plan. It means you recognise that you have a chance to find another way of doing things.

So where do you think you sit on the scale of openness and vulnerability? I've taken the guesswork out of it an created the Vulnerability Test so you can literally see what your score is!

Mark 0 for every Yes response
Mark 1 for every No response

- ⓢ Do I hide things about myself for fear of being judged by others?
- ⓢ Do I cover things up when I am wrong?
- ⓢ Do I avoid asking for help?
- ⓢ Do I feel jealous of people with confidence?
- ⓢ Do I take criticism to heart?
- ⓢ Do I hide my true feelings when asked?
- ⓢ Do I hate being asked questions about myself?
- ⓢ Do I only share my highlight real with the world?
- ⓢ Have I settled for less?
- ⓢ Do I hide my emotions from people?

What is your score?

0-3 – You are closed off!
Trust me when I say vulnerability and a strong sense of self-worth are directly linked to the future success of your career or business, so don't stuff around on this! It's time to get help to build yourself up.

4-6 – You're doing okay.
Continue to dedicate time and energy to building your sense of self-worth. Greater vulnerability can be achieved

by becoming more confident in who you are and what you bring to the world.

8-9 – Almost there…
You are making great headway with being open and vulnerable. The goal is just around the next bend. See how you can take your dedication to authenticity to the next level.

10 – You have reached peak vulnerability!
You are ready to make your authentic mark on the world.

CHAPTER 8
MONEY

As you know, I started my business with a base of $500 per week. This was money for my family, not to spend on my business. In reality, I had a zero budget to start my business. For some people, that's a huge barrier, and they can't get past the idea that you can absolutely start a business with no savings and build it up to one that pulls in seven figures.

It's called bootstrapping, baby. There are money-savvy ways to do just about everything when you are starting up. My customer relationship management (CRM) system was a basic Excel spreadsheet that I updated whenever I was on the phone to a client. I recorded every single one of my enquiries and interactions and built up a database of almost 40,000 in four years. Yes, it takes work, but I knew that if I wasn't prepared to put in the work, I may as well go back to being an employee!

I would sit down with a list of follow-up calls to do and smash them out in a half hour window, updating the client notes on Excel as I went. I didn't allow myself to ever procrastinate on even the small things like that, because let's face it, it's lazy to think you'll go back and do it later – you probably won't. Of course, there were things at the beginning that I didn't like, but anyone who starts something with nothing has to do all of "the things" until such time as you can pay someone else to do the things that you don't get excited about.

My answering service was the standard mobile phone voicemail. My automation software was whatever had a basic, free offer.

I was the whiteboard queen and wrote up all of the résumés I had on the go, when they were due, as well as where the career consulting clients were in their process. Systematically, I knew where I was at all times.

Any customer notes I recorded started with Excel. With no money to pay for a proper CRM, this was my only option. I sent out an email once a week to maintain consistency and would cut and paste the email column of my Excel spreadsheet to blind cc (carbon copy) to everyone. Consistency is all about credibility. If you send one email and never contact your list again, it doesn't look like you are the real deal. To me, a sporadic approach means you are giving off fraud vibes.

Organic social media was my friend. It's free! You don't even need a website to start a business, just a business page on social media platforms where people can find reviews and information about you and see that you are consistently posting. This is how you build credibility, my friend!

I looked for free platforms where I could list my business and contact details and wasn't afraid to openly ask people if they knew a friend or family member who needed my services. You can't be backwards about being forward when you have a business to build. That simple question can transform a business by building momentum.

But when it was just me and I was driven by a vision to build a business I could be proud of and that would empower people to pursue careers they were passionate about, I didn't have room for "I'll do it later." If I had that attitude, I would have been stuffed. You need to get stuck in and get your hands dirty, it takes grit, determination, and resilience in spades.

I began to be able to pay myself at the end of May, four weeks after I went into KLCC full-time, and then hired my first assistant in

September. But the reality is that the very first thing I invested in was basic systems, like Office 365, and the ability to create some funnels and automation so I could build my reach. I started off spending $20 a day on social media ads, and now it's up around $1,500 a day. I also invest over $1,500 a month on my automation system and another $200 a month on *ClickFunnels* for the fourteen ways in which I can draw in new clients. I'm a bit addicted to it, but I get so much joy from hearing a new voice at the end of the phone when they've found us through those systems.

I'm all about accessibility and authenticity, so there are absolutely still times when I man the phones and make calls, and people seem shocked when I answer the phone. But why shouldn't you remain hands-on in your business, even when you have built a team around you to support your vision? To me, automation is a great tool for me to touch more people; it's not an excuse for me to be lazy.

The new-found sense of self-worth I'd found at the retreat carried over into everything related to my personal life and my business. When setting my initial prices, I charged $199 for the full résumé service, which was usually a good solid few hours of work. When it came to choosing a rate for my new coaching service, I was loaded with imposter syndrome – you know, where you feel like even though you have extensive experience in an industry, you don't believe that you are worth that much?

I wondered whether I could charge $199 an hour for career coaching. Boy, did my mind have some shit to say about that idea... *I can't charge that much! I don't have a piece of paper that says I can do this!*

Here's where things get sticky, right?

> When I can't see my own worth, it's because I have a misconception of what I bring to the table.

I had to get out of my own way. So here are the facts:

1. I had fifteen years of experience in recruitment and had worked in many different areas, so my knowledge was well-rounded.
2. I was often the top performer in any role I took on.
3. I advanced quickly within other people's businesses because I was a dedicated hard worker.
4. My clients recognised the value I provided for them.
5. I had a Diploma of Human Resources, Diploma of Counselling, and Diploma of Management.

Okay, Kate, what's the worst that can happen? You charge $199 an hour for coaching and people aren't willing to pay it. Can you handle that? YES! I'd either have to look for a different clientele or lower my starting price and build up from there.

Alright, $199 it is!

Following the retreat, I created a Career Accelerator Program that took my career coaching to a whole new level. I won a business award for fast achievement and was up on stage with some of the most influential people in business. I had never doubted my own ability to achieve anything I set my mind to, but I had been carrying a chip on my shoulder for most of my young life around being worthy. As I stood up on that stage, bottle of Moet in one hand and a framed certificate in the other, I finally felt like their equal, like I deserved to be up there with them.

I was firmly operating in my genius zone. I have never been a perfectionist and have always been a doer.

 I believe done is better than perfect.

If you think about things for too long or spend time questioning yourself, it can hinder your progress. The answer? Trust your gut. How much time have you wasted on projects or activities because you want to get everything "right" before you execute? I get it, but it's really not worth it. Just get in and get it done.

As my sense of self-worth increased, it began to match my unwavering self-belief, and I became unstoppable. The value I placed on my time has grown over the years since then. While I used to cringe about putting $199 on my résumé services or asking for the same price for every hour of career coaching, I went up to $297, then $397. As my team grew throughout 2021, this was the rate I charged to have one of my capable team members work with clients, and I would charge an extra $200 if they wanted to work directly with me. So at that stage, my minimum hourly rate was $597.

In 2022, I was approached by the National Disability Insurance Scheme (NDIS) to conduct a workshop for over one hundred people to take them through writing résumés and going through job interviews. I could stand there and talk about this all day, so it was an easy "Yes" for me to accept the offer. They offered me $2000 for a ninety-minute presentation. When you are in your genius zone and getting momentum, it just flows.

When I began Kate Langford Business Consulting (KLBC) in 2023 – a story I'll share later in this book – my minimum hourly rate was $1,000. Yes, I took it to a whole new level, but that is because I know without a doubt what I bring to the table. I know how quickly I can cut through the shit so my clients can address the things that really matter in order to skyrocket their business systematically and correctly without being overwhelmed.

I value my time so much more now, and I consider every hour that I spend as a precious commodity. Because my why is my family,

I have to weigh up what an hour away from them is worth. Sounds blunt, right? But when I take the value outside of myself and make it about my why, it shows just how valuable my time is.

There's always a period of test and measure when it comes to pricing. If there are too many people instantly saying "Yes," it's too low. If there are too many people with a hard "No," it's too high. It was a real knuckle-biter for me to pitch that price of $1,000 to one of my first KLBC clients, but the moment they said "Yes," I knew I had hit the sweet spot. It was high enough to make them just a little nervous but got them enough skin in the game that they would take it seriously.

As you know, I did not start my business to be a millionaire, so even when the business started to grow faster than I had ever imagined it could, the bucks have not been the be-all and end-all for me. Anyone who goes out to start a business to make lots of money is forgetting the real reason. That's just my belief. A lot of people will disagree with that, that's cool, but I feel if you start a business because you want to make a lot of money, there will be a ceiling. However, when you do something for passion, and it evolves, as long as you can pay yourself, there is no limit to where you can take it.

And guess what? It will be way more fulfilling to focus on how you can be of service rather than how you can make a quick buck.

Gold Nuggets for Money

One of the first concepts I introduce to my Career Accelerator Program participants is Success Equals.

In a nutshell, it means that everyone's definition of success is different. For some, it's money; for others, it's an abundance of time; for some, it's awards; and for others, it's a full calendar of clients.

There is no right or wrong, but it's important to be aware of what success equals for you. I've never measured success against the number of zeros in my account; success has always equalled doing something I am passionate about.

I've always been hungry for success, even as an employee. For me then, it was still not about the money; it was about being the best in that role in the business. I wanted to be the best recruitment coordinator, the best consultant, the best manager... whatever the role was.

I was measuring success by the number of temps (people I had working for me), the number of candidates I placed into jobs, or the dollars brought into the company I was working for. Back then, my success depended on how I ranked in comparison to my peers (Yes, I can be slightly competitive...). I was then single and working fourteen-hour days to make my numbers the best they could be. When I had eighty-eight temps in the Queensland Police Service, I was on cloud nine. When I was bringing in

$40,000 a month in revenue for a previous employer and was their top salesperson, I felt pumped.

But guess what? That has completely shifted now. Success to me equals being able to relax if I'm going through the supermarket checkout and I have hungry kids who require $400 worth of healthy groceries and I don't have to worry about swiping that card. Success for me means I can get to my kids' sports days and be able to schedule in family holidays and everything is still running fine in the office without me. Success to me means that I can pay for activities for my family without freaking out that the dent I've made in the account won't be refilled. Those are the core things I measure myself against to determine if I am being successful.

Even as a businesswoman, I don't measure myself against my bank balance. My success is no longer a comparison game; it is measured against myself only. How I feel, how I show up, how fulfilling my work is. That's how simple it can be.

There's no argument that money management is vital to ensure the sustainability and longevity of your business, so here are some tips to strengthen this area up for you:

- ⓢ Pay yourself from day one. Even if it is less some weeks, it is key to have a wage starting out.

- ⓢ Price rises are key to keep on top of, especially as demand goes up.

- ⓢ Marketing should be the last thing in your budget to be cut – without leads, you have no business.

- ⓢ Take calculated risks when it comes to money.
- ⓢ Always pay bills as soon as they come in so you have a clear picture of your finances.
- ⓢ Have bars to measure your break-even point.
- ⓢ Know when you can afford a new team member.
- ⓢ Know how much you can spend on "wants" without taking away from the "needs."

CHAPTER 9
GROWTH

Within a year, I brought résumé writing back onshore because KLCC was doing brilliantly. We had two résumé writers, and I had hired another career consultant to assist me with the volume of clients, which was growing. I was doing about $10,000 a month at that stage.

My first hire was doing brilliantly. She started part-time for one day a week and quickly moved up to full-time. She learned everything about my business and could run it just as well as I could. She had implemented business processes to help things to run more smoothly and treated my business as her own. I thought I had done a brilliant job of choosing the perfect person who would stay with me long term. It's an employer's dream... until it wasn't.

It was close to twelve months after I hired my first team member when something shifty was brought to my attention. I had placed so much faith and belief in her and was devastated to learn this had been going on for some time behind my back. While I was angry, I was equal parts scared. She knew my business inside and out; in fact, there were some areas where she knew more than I did, because I had let her create systems to improve her workflow while I stayed in my genius zone of coaching and bringing clients in.

I rang Dad in an absolute panic.

"What am I going to do? She knows everything!"

"You'll do the right thing for you, Kate."

"Yeah, but do I keep her on so that I keep the processes in place? What will happen if I let her go and everything turns to shit?"

Dad was supportive as always and encouraged me to take some time to sit with it.

I've always found it interesting how I am a highly emotional person, but when it comes to business decisions, I am usually able to take a deep breath and disconnect from emotion and move into risk-versus-reward mode to make a logical decision. Because she was my first hire, I had taken this disloyalty as a personal insult. I was stuck in my emotions. This would have been an easy problem for me to solve for an employer if it came across my desk while working in recruitment. It was time to move into Business Kate mode.

When I did, I was able to weigh everything up with a clear head.

Okay, so she knows some areas of my business that I don't – that's on me. I need to take more ownership of how everything is done in my business. Okay, that lesson is on board. Now, what to do? I could keep her on so that I don't have the emotional stress and worry. The problem with that is that I can no longer trust her, and that is so important to me. I need to be able to completely trust anyone in my team. It also goes against my integrity and values to work alongside someone who is dishonest. What is the risk? If I let her go, I might lose some momentum while I figure out new systems, rehire someone else, and train them up. If I don't let her go, I will be out of alignment and will probably start to micromanage and be looking over her shoulder every few seconds to make sure she doesn't slip up again. Is that going to be the best use of my time? Hell no! I have lives to change.

Can I find someone else? It may take time, but there is definitely a better fit out there for me. Take the risk, let her go. Someone better is out there.

I could have kept her on for safety reasons, but integrity and morals are so important for me. I was still scared when I took her out the back of my house and had to let her go, but I trusted that by making the right decision for myself, it would all work out.

I learned *a huge* lesson that while it's important to delegate tasks to make operations more efficient, I should never lose sight of how things are done in my business. I have to know the processes that are in place, even if I'm not hands-on with that particular area. I am grateful that I learned that lesson in my first year of business and not my fifth. I pledged to never let one person know everything in my business – not even me, because if I were to be unavailable for weeks on end, my team would not be able to operate without me.

I'm not going to lie, I was a little challenged in looking a new team member. I had just been burned by the first person I had placed my trust in. But I still had my grand vision to bring to life, so I had to put my big girl pants on and get the back into it. There was no time to have a pity party.

At that stage, I had Leroy in prep every day, and Gracie was at kindy Monday, Wednesday, and Thursday. Leroy went to after-school care on Monday, Wednesday, and Thursday, so I could have three full days at work. Tuesday and Fridays were girls' days, and I would hang out with Gracie so we could have that one-on-one time. I tried to keep the weekends for myself – it's really important to do that – but as you can appreciate, while growing a business, I had to be available. One thing I pride myself on is efficiency, so I always get back to clients. I've put in the hard yards to be able to get that reputation of people appreciating me getting back to them.

In September 2019, an angel called Lisa walked into my office. She was a friend who had offered to come into the business to help me out short term. She would go on to become my right-hand woman for three years in KLCC. She set about implementing and documenting processes so they could become a part of future team training.

By that stage, I had hired a career coach, and it was a relief to know I had my core team of three locked in and solid, especially since I had found out I was pregnant! This was the third child I had hoped to manifest when Jay and I built the fourth bedroom into our home almost eighteen months earlier.

While my belly was growing, the business was growing faster. I went from $10,000 a month to $20,000 and then $30,000 within a matter of six months. By the end of 2019, we hit $40,000 months, and I had almost grown my business tenfold since the retreat just a year earlier. It was insane growth, and I was so fortunate that my third pregnancy was a drama-free one.

Unfortunately, I couldn't say the same about the labour.

My wish for a smooth birth after two horrific ones just did not come to pass. Our third child was due in late January. I went into hospital with contractions on 28 January. I tried really hard to have a natural birth. I wanted so desperately to be able to birth my baby and have that special bonding moment of skin-to-skin that I hadn't had with my eldest two.

I got to eight centimetres dilation myself, and then things seemed to come to a standstill. I was in all sorts of pain for twenty-four hours, as labour dragged on and on without any progress in the dilation department. I was so determined for a natural birth that I held out and weathered it all. After a day, it was the midwife who called time. She said I would have to go in for a C-section as I'd been labouring for too long.

"Just give me a little bit longer, please?" I was scrambling, because I could see my dream slipping away once more.

"Sorry, dear, we have to do this to keep you and the baby safe."

They wheeled me into surgery, and they opened me up to find another ten-pound boy. His head had been stuck. There was no way he was going to come out on his own, and things would have been quite dire if the midwife had let me go for longer as I'd asked. The surgeon had to do an extra cut to get him out, and I lost a lot of blood as a result. I was hooked up for a blood transfusion while my baby was whisked away to get monitored.

I didn't get to push on 30 January 2020, but I was grateful that our Lincoln was a big, healthy boy. We were able to bring him home after four days.

It was only when I was coming out of my baby bubble that I realised Lisa and my team had been facing something absolutely devastating for the business... Every single one of our thirteen Facebook ads had been shut down the very same day I had gone into labour. I had no idea, because Lisa hadn't wanted to bother me with it. Instead, she rolled her sleeves up and got to work fixing the problem. What a legend!

Losing social media advertising might not seem like the end of the world, but let me paint a picture for you. Facebook was the only source driving people to my business at that time. Those thirteen ads were bringing in sixty leads a day. They were powerful enough to encourage those sixty people to give us their email addresses so we could nurture them. We had organic reach, sure, but the only marketing I was paying for was on social media, and it was designed to drive new people we hadn't connected to yet through the funnel to make a phone call and become clients.

Something had triggered the alarm bells at Facebook HQ, and they had restricted the business account, which shut down every single one of the funnels we had operating. It was an error, but being an international business like Facebook, it was hard for KLCC and my team to crack through the barriers in place to get it resolved. They worked around the clock for nights on end, twenty-four hours a day, with consultants in the USA to get it back. We eventually lost the whole account, but my team created a new account to get the algorithms back up again, literally setting it all up once more from scratch. If you know how complicated social media marketing systems are, you will appreciate just how much work goes into this. It was most impressive that they were able to take on that kind of project so I could remain in my blissful ignorance and enjoy our newest addition to the family.

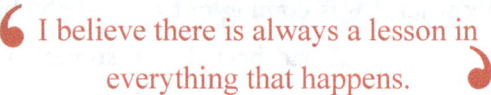

> I believe there is always a lesson in everything that happens.

So, what was the lesson here? Don't put all of your eggs in one basket when it comes to reaching and converting new clients. I now use multiple channels, including traditional and non-traditional media, to boost the presence of the businesses.

When something goes wrong, there is a two-step process I go through: I pause and think, *What do I need to do to solve the problem? Then what do I need to fix so it doesn't happen again?* Just solving the problem is not enough; it's important in business to plug those gaps and fix the source of any glitches as they arise so that they don't come back and get ya. It is a constant dance between growth and consolidation as you put new processes in place and strengthen the "old" ones.

In the midst all of this, a new virus called Covid-19 was being talked about overseas. Only a few weeks after we brought Lincoln home, it was on Australian shores, and there were talks about closing international and interstate borders to try to stop it from spreading. There was a whirlwind of uncertainty, and fear was creeping in for many of the business owners I knew.

While many businesses chose to downsize, lay off staff, and cut all marketing spending, I leaned into the hurricane and kept things steady. I didn't want my team to lose their jobs, and there was no way I was going to let KLCC go down without a fight. My fears looked like they were going to take hold when we finished February with a twenty percent dip in turnover at around $6,000. It was not dire, but it was enough for me to do my best to keep panic at bay.

I didn't have the knee-jerk reaction others had during those times. Instead of cutting one of my team members, I spent more on advertising. The most unexpected thing happened – instead of going down any further, growth hit KLCC like a freight train.

By March 2020, we hit our first $50,000 month, and then it rapidly grew to $80,000. KLCC officially became a million-dollar business in the middle of a global pandemic. It was an incredibly exciting time for me, but it was intense. There I was, with a newborn baby and two other kids under six, having to hire new team members at a rapid pace in order to grow our capacity to meet the booming demand. By April 2020, KLCC had a team of nine that included consultants, a personal assistant and my right hand – who was essentially another me – along with another three subcontractors who wrote résumés.

Things were going gangbusters, and while I tried my best to guide the team from home, there came a time when I had to roll my sleeves up and head back to captain the ship two days a week. We were out in unchartered waters, and although the winds were in our favour, without strong leadership, there was every chance the ship could veer off course and we could end up on the rocks.

Lincoln was four months old when I went back to work two days a week, but I have no regrets about it. It was my time to truly wear all of the hats and wear them with presence and focus. It was time to prove to myself that I truly could have it all. There is a photo that nails the feels of this point in time – Lincoln sitting on Lisa's lap while we are having a strategy meeting at the desk in my office.

Did I put being a mother on hold? No. Did I decide we had to wind down the business because we couldn't keep up? No. When Lincoln was awake, I tended to what he needed and gave him my all, and the moment he went down for a nap, I would be interviewing new candidates for a consultant role or working through my to-do list.

Being able to be present for a single task or role at any given time, that is the key to having it all. It's real, and it is possible. I know because that was when I was truly able to embody that belief. The business was going crazy, and I went with it. I didn't hold back. I didn't hold the business back. The "Go" button had been hit by people who needed to find new job opportunities or move from careers in areas like hospitality and travel that had been absolutely smashed by Covid. These were people who had to look at how they could transfer skills into completely different industries ASAP in order to keep a roof over their heads and food on the table for their families. There was no way I could press the "Stop" button if that was what was going on in the world and I had a business that could help.

It takes a team to make that happen, though. Jay was getting up for Lincoln in the night so I could get eight hours of sleep and be ready to power through the next day. Did I have guilt around that? No, because I could see how important it was for me to be firing on all cylinders. Lincoln was still getting everything he needed, and he has a beautiful bond with his dad now as a result.

The team also stepped it up so we could keep the momentum going as well as meet the needs of the people who jumped on board our train.

> **If I had hesitated, even for a moment, the train would have left the station without us.**

But I was so ready to roll. We were not passengers on some random train; KLCC had our own service line, and I was the driver.

We hit our biggest month ever in June 2021, at $100,000. And this was a month I was not even in the office! This meant so much to me, because it was a true testament to the way that I led my team, the way we connected, and the way that each and every single one of them owned this business like it's their baby.

Going into July, I realised as we were scaling and spending $1,500 to $1,700 a day on Facebook ads that we were getting between forty and fifty calls a day. We tried to hire a few different consultants, but most of them never worked out, because the culture fit or the consultant element wasn't there. By the time August rolled around, I realised the business didn't have the processes in place to scale. I didn't have the people, the structure, or the systems in place to do that and realised that it couldn't grow effectively without any of those.

Lisa had come to me and said that she wasn't able to continue with the hours because she wanted to go back to university. It was too much for one person to do, especially managing nine people, five résumé writers, and systems that were growing. This was the big eye-opener, and I decided to restructure the whole business mid-August 2022, and that took its toll on me personally. We moved team positions around and decided to fix the CRM system so that it could do everything we wanted in one place rather than using Excel spreadsheets.

You might think that the excitement of building so quickly and seeing the money rolling in is thrilling, and it is to an extent, but it began to concern me when it went on for a decent period of time.

I was recruiting constantly, but the problem with looking for new people when you already need them is that it rushes the process. Not all of the people I chose in my haste were the right fit for KLCC, and some did not last for long with the expansion happening all around us. While it felt like the rest of the country was slowing its pace, ours was kicking into high gear, and the difference between the two didn't align with some of my new recruits.

I saw so many businesses fall, and it didn't make sense that we weren't facing similar challenges. It reached a point where I didn't want to talk about my business to anyone outside of my team, because I was to empathetic to how devastating that twelve-month window was for so many others. Businesses were downsizing, scaling back, and even closing down, while mine was on course for the stratosphere.

I handled the growth by recruiting. Again, I learned from that experience. Being ahead of the game is important, and it is rare that you won't see a "We're hiring" ad from me now, because I am constantly on the hunt for good team members. When I am approached by people who want to work for KLCC, I don't turn them down. I hear them out and see if they are a good fit for the team. If they are a perfect match, I will find a role for them or keep them in mind if I can't stretch to fit them at the time. That way, when a position does open up, I have a shortlist of vetted candidates already waiting for me.

I handled the growth by putting in longer hours alongside my team. It was intense, I'm not going to lie, but I set myself "hustle blocks" and would schedule them in. Yes, it was a time for hustle. When you are in a phase of constant, rapid growth, you have to. There are so many people who think "hustle" is a dirty word.

I agree that hustle is not sustainable, but it is necessary.

Without it, you simply cannot run a successful business. The difference is, I have a *deadline* for hustle. I don't stay in that mode 24/7 for months on end. A deadline is critical, because the people who do not have one end up burned out, and then they are no good to anyone. Having a deadline for hustle not only makes you more productive, but it gives you a light at the end of the tunnel that you can look forward to reaching.

It took many conversations to clear the way for me to do that. I didn't just put my head down and block out my other responsibilities. I set myself a three-week hustle block, with Jay and the kids' blessing. During that block, I worked late nights to simplify processes in order to make the workflow more seamless and reduce the time I would need to spend training new recruits. I spent countless hours with my team, moving our backend systems from free platforms onto paid systems that would help to streamline everything and enhance automation.

I handled the growth by evolving. KLCC really had a facelift during Covid, and that made it so much easier to scale. This would not have been possible without a hustle block. I launched a brand new Career Changers Academy Membership to enable me to engage with more people at a cheaper price point.

The word pivot, which I absolutely hate but was on the tip of everyone's tongue during Covid, was everywhere.

 In business, it's important to make sure you are across what the market needs at any given moment.

With so much uncertainty and people being made redundant left, right, and centre, people didn't have much money. The Career Changers

Academy allowed me to reach more people with each touchpoint, and this reduced the cost for them to participate; it was a win-win. It was incredibly successful, and people were eager to be able to learn from me and pick my brains at our weekly virtual meetings.

Once I achieved everything I set out to in that three-week block, I pulled back into my more balanced lifestyle, knowing that I had been productive and focused intensely to have maximum results in that time. Of course, 2020–21 required multiple hustle blocks in order for us to make it through.

I managed to get through those few years, but it remains – by far – both the hardest and most successful growth period of KLCC as I write this book. As much as I manifest and believe anything is possible, I am also a realist when it comes to business, and I knew there was only so long we could keep going at that pace before we reached a plateau. After a while, I *wanted* it to calm down.

For me, consistency is better than rapid growth. It is key to allow you to consolidate everything and ensure it is all running smoothly. My wish for consistency was granted for twelve months throughout 2022, and in 2023, I hit *go* for the next level of growth.

Gold Nuggets for Growth

A key lesson in being able to grow your business is being okay with delegation and letting go. I was more than happy to palm off the areas of KLCC that I found myself procrastinating on, but there was another level of challenge for me when I realised I had to start delegating other things I didn't hate in the name of being able to grow the business.

I am only one person, after all.

Even before KLCC blasted into the rapid growth phase of 2020, hiring new team members was not the easiest thing for me to do, because I have a certain way of doing things. We all do, right? I believed there was no one who could be as efficient at some things as I could be, and it would just be easier to do it myself than to be disappointed if someone else did it and they did it wrong. I see so many businesswomen get stuck at this point; they cannot scale and grow, because they are not willing to let go.

Trust me, I know having those perfectionist issues is very challenging. When I stepped back and ran a risk-versus-reward analysis, I knew the only way I could grow was to get help on board. It meant that I could stay in my genius zone, and I could find people who had genius zones that took care of my weaknesses.

Get that journal out and answer these:

- Ⓢ What are the things I love doing?
- Ⓢ What can't I stand doing?
- Ⓢ What am I prepared to let go of?
- Ⓢ Where is a major area of growth I can see emerging and how can I prepare for it?
- Ⓢ Where are resources being underutilised that I could make better use of?
- Ⓢ What are the priorities for future growth?

CHAPTER 10
HEALTH

Having it all means bringing your health into the picture. I'm not just talking about your physical health but also mental well-being. In my pursuit to have it all in 2020, I kept my business and family in balance with the hustle blocks, but my health began to slip.

As a person who loved sport, I was not exercising. I did not have anything for myself outside of work and home life, and I was teetering on a nervous breakdown from having to constantly climb up ladders to put out metaphorical fires in my world.

This is why this book is in your hands right now. If you haven't already experienced burnout for yourself, I am so happy for you! But you would be a rare unicorn! The way we are conditioned to think about being a businesswoman means we can unknowingly steer ourselves in the direction of burnout from the moment we become entrepreneurs. We are conditioned to think that we have to do it all and be the best at everything, but I have learned (the hard way) that you don't have to do either of those things. In fact, when you don't strive for perfection and doing it all, you can have it all, because you focus on the right things, and your health is right up there at the top.

As a mum who wanted to have it all, outsourcing became my best friend at home as well. I had been doing it since 2018 in my business, but the borderline burnout of 2020 led me to turn my attention to what I could outsource at home in order to free up more time for me to be with my kids.

In 2021, I decided to hire a nanny one day a week. When I looked into the cost (risk versus reward), I realised that I could pay a highly skilled person a couple of hundred dollars to come in on a Friday to care for Lincoln, pick up the kids from school, help with the washing, and even mop the floors if Lincoln went down for a nap. This is where knowing your hourly rate is critical!

I was charging my time out at $397 an hour for career consulting at the time, so it made financial sense for me to make that investment once a week. If I were to continue doing all of those chores, and say it took me two hours, it would cost me almost $800 to "pay myself" to mop the floors and do washing. That's money I would not want to spend. But I could free myself up for those two hours to potentially make four times what I would invest in having those chores done for me so I could be with the kids. Win-win!

Mopping and washing are not things I am emotionally invested in, so they can go. There are some things I won't let go of, like cooking. I *love* cooking for my family. Even on my craziest days, I will still have something prepared for dinner. It's a non-negotiable for me. It is soul-filling for me to know that I am putting my love into nourishing my family, and that time in the kitchen allows me to decompress and focus on creating something from nothing – my happy place.

There are certain things that you don't let go of because they light you up. All of the things that you procrastinate on or things that need to be routinely done to keep things functioning but don't specifically need you to do them, they can be outsourced. It is something to seriously consider when you are growing and need to be more conscious of where you spend your time.

Having our nanny helped to relieve the pressure to keep up the housework.

> ❛ It was a great lesson to understand that *having it all* doesn't necessarily mean doing it all.

Learning to accept help in all its forms is one of the quickest ways to have it all.

As you know, I have been a driven, independent woman my whole life, but even I had to learn when to tap out. There's no point in continuing to push through and do everything when there are capable people around us who are willing and able to help, either as paid professionals or as unpaid personal supporters.

When it comes to my mental well-being, I have fucking worked my arse off on personal growth and development. I learned early on in my business journey that I would never be able to push through the shit and achieve everything I had envisioned if I was still anchored in crap from decades ago. We carry it all with us, you know. My divorce, the skydiving accident, the emergency C-sections, even the feeling of being sidelined in the schoolyard; I carried it all.

I have seen psychologists for years, because as much as I am all about learning all I can to run a successful business, I also understand the power of learning all I can about myself. I have read self-development books and listened to podcasts about the power of the mind and how to blast through negativity. I love the work of no-nonsense thought leaders like Ant Middleton and David Goggins. Their authentic hardness and the ethos of getting stuck in and doing the fucking work without complaining and feeling like the victim is spot on.

You know I'm a firm believer in how everything in life is a *choice*. There's a concept I have learned that distinguishes between whether you think like a victor or a victim. It comes with a simple question, "Are you above or below the line?" You always have a choice.

Those who have a victor mindset and are "above the line" take ownership of themselves, are accountable for their actions, and take responsibility for how they show up in the world. Those who are victims sit "below the line" and blame others, make excuses, and sit firmly in denial. It's a very powerful concept to anchor into your psyche. Share it with everyone you know! Whenever I hear Jay making an excuse about something, I simply ask, "Jay, are you below the line?" and it's enough to snap him out of it. And he holds me equally accountable.

I have been through a lot, but I had a choice on how I moved on from each incident. I could choose to stay stuck in the shit, or I could get the bloody hose out to wash it off, learn how to avoid the pile next time, and then move on. We always have a choice, which is why I am frustrated by people who are negative or keep presenting themselves as a victim because they choose to stay there. I didn't, so I don't have a lot of time for those people. That's really harsh, but it's true. I've done the work, and so can anyone. There are just those who choose not to.

Experiences can change people – if you choose to let them. I could have chosen to remain the victim and lived out my life without following any of my dreams. But I chose to get the most out of life. I don't want to live an average, *così così* life. I want to be something. We get one life. I could die tomorrow, and I'm cool with that, because today, I'm living the hell out of it.

I have had to go on a journey of acceptance, and believe me when I say it has not been smooth sailing. As you know, I was bullied at school. In Year 6, we used to play handball, and there were always four starting positions: the ace at the top, followed by the king, the queen, and then the dunce. I had enough going for me that I would get to hang out with the cool kids, but there were compromises I had to make, like always being the dunce. Like getting everyone's tuckshop orders for them and delivering it to them at our hangout spot. Like being the person who always supported everyone else, never being seen or heard myself.

It meant I was always a follower, always just hanging onto the tail end of what the cool kids were. Even though I was great at sport and even had a hot boyfriend by the end of high school, it wasn't enough for me to really assert myself. This affected my friendships for many years. I felt like I had to work for everything and was always worrying what people thought about me. I made a choice to continue to believe that I was not good enough to have friends who truly supported me and had my back.

Being someone who has high emotional intelligence coupled with a brain that runs at lightning speed, I can fall into the habit of mind chatter, always analysing how people might interpret what I say or do. Believe me, the stories are not flattering. I would create two or three different stories from one single interaction with someone. That is the power of the mind at work! It all comes back to that sense of "otherness" for me.

But I have made a choice. Staying in my own head was blocking me from connecting with other people – especially women – and I had to find a way out of that mind chatter so I could free up that mental space and use it more productively.

Cognitive behaviour therapy (CBT) has been amazing for me. I love this stuff. That is why I did a Diploma of Counselling before I started my business for no reason other than I love the way the human brain works and wanted to learn more about it. CBT gave me some incredible insights on how I can stop a story from unfolding in my head. It means I have the tools to be able to stop it in its tracks. "Okay, Kate, you are being emotionally hijacked right now – where is the evidence that this story is true?" It brings me back to my logical mind. When I take the emotion away and look at the facts, I can see clear as day that this story is a fabrication.

Working with a psychologist in the lead-up to starting my business also helped me to get clear on what my true focus is. I understood that as long as I have my family under one roof with me, then all is right in my world. Anyone else who comes on the journey with me, I will give everything to so long as they reciprocate, whereas when I was younger, I would give everything to anyone so long as they would allow me to go on a journey with them.

See how powerful of a switch that is?

I am no longer allowing people to take the piss while I get burned out. I haven't closed off; rather, I have a strong understanding of who I am. I also *like* who I am. That is huge! Freeing up my mental capacity has elevated the way that I coach. I attract the right people, because I have tapped into my intuition and my gut, and people can feel my sense of self-assuredness. I am prepared to say "No" to any potential client with whom I do not feel aligned. I get a sense, even on our first call together, whether someone will work well with my energy or not. It is powerful to know that you can actually turn people away! When you have an abundance mindset, you understand that you are not depriving yourself of income when you say "No." If you feel that, you are anchored in scarcity.

With an abundance mindset, you know that by saying "No" to someone who isn't the right fit for you, you are clearing the way for the right person to come in.

> ❛ Sometimes, a single "No" to a person who is not a great fit can lead to multiple ideal clients coming in! ❜

The same could be said for personal relationships. For every person who drains you, there are others waiting in the wings who can uplift you. When you say no to the "drainer," you make space for an "uplifter" to enter your world. It's like the universe is doing a sneaky test on you to see if you are still remaining true to your values and boundaries.

I have a healer that I see whenever I feel like I'm starting to get mentally frazzled, and as 2022 progressed, I began to build a Kate Day into my week. I share more about this in the Balance chapter, but in a nutshell, it is my own sacred day. I have also been known to see a psychic from time to time, without any outcome in mind, as a chance to tap into a higher power to see if what I think and feel is in alignment. Having it all means ensuring you have a holistic approach to mental health.

If there is an area of life I am struggling with, I will find an audiobook that is going to give me some juice around that. Maybe it's a single word or one line that I'll take away from that audiobook, but I know the universe has sent me what I need to connect with.

My radar is constantly on, so being in touch with my emotional self is critical, because it allows me to filter out anything that doesn't resonate with me and on the things that do. If something is not right for me, I know immediately, and I'll move away. This creates strong boundaries that serve me well personally and professionally. It means I don't say "Yes" to anything and everything. I can just as readily say "No," because I will feel if something is not right for me.

Remember how I used to struggle with being alone, especially when I fled to London? I can happily be alone with myself and my thoughts for days at a time now. Honouring how I feel has allowed me to elevate my business faster and faster, because I do whatever my soul needs at any given moment. If I wake up and feel like shit, or even just have a sense that I'm not operating at a top level and there's a crap day ahead, I will have a shower to try to cleanse the energy.

As the water runs over me, I'll assess: "What can I do to control this situation?" If there are things I can actively do to shift my mental state, I will do it. If not, I might choose to sit that one out. I don't try to slap myself out of the slump and push through. I will surrender for an hour or even a twenty-four-hour period of flatness and let everything take its natural course. Being able to do this has heightened my ability to stay true to my intuition.

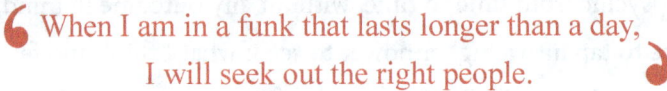

> When I am in a funk that lasts longer than a day, I will seek out the right people.

If I need motivation, I will go to someone who can give me a verbal kick up the arse. If I need someone to listen, I will go to someone who can say, "That really sucks," without feeling compelled to fix it for me. If I don't want company at all, I will be happy sitting with myself and might even sit down and watch a movie in the middle of the day on a Kate Day if that's what I need.

When it comes to physical health, I believe our body is a machine for the soul. I feel I am looking after my physicality in order for my soul to be able to do its work. There are many ways to view who we are as humans, but I believe our bodies and our emotional souls are two different components. If one fails, the other will, too; it is just a matter of time.

To stay firing on all cylinders, you have to take care of the body so your soul can thrive, and you have to take care of your soul so you have the motivation and energy to fuel your body.

You have a sense of how driven I am. Well, I was a competitive sportswoman, too! You know I competed in cross-country, netball, and discus in high school. After school, I took up softball and continue playing netball to this day. Sport can be a mental game, especially when you work your body so hard that it starts to hurt, but I had a strong mental will from a young age. I don't know many other primary-school youngsters who were as devoted to writing motivational mantras and sticking them on their bedroom walls as I was!

After my divorce and hiatus in London, I stopped competing. I had to rebuild my emotional state, so the spotlight was on healing my broken heart and quelling the anxiety that had welled up in me as a result of the abrupt end to my marriage. My physical being was left untended to. I wasn't exercising or playing sport. Instead, I was emotionally eating, and I drank every day, as was the lifestyle in inner-city London. I put on weight, and those habits stuck with me for years.

Although I drank less when I came back to Australia, I didn't do much physical activity, and by 2012, I had put on weight. I had three babies between then and 2021, when I was at my heaviest. After having Gracie in 2015, I started to move my body more. I'd go for walks with the kids, and running around after Leroy as a toddler kept me active, but it wasn't enough. I became a mother who was there for everyone else. I didn't really have my outlet – which was my work – that I really loved, because recruitment had lost its shine for me by then. Looking back, I realised the spark wasn't there, so I had no motivation in me to take care of my body.

When I started KLCC, my spark came back. I found that love for my work again, and it was the catalyst for me to change my physical well-being. *Now that I'm feeling the energy and love for my work, I'm finding the love for myself.*

I can say hand-on-heart that I now don't have a single bloody regret in my life. But at that time, there was one niggling at me – I didn't like what I was looking at in the mirror. I was a size twenty after I had Lincoln and was frustrated that I had let my health lapse for so long. It was time to fix that once and for all!

I gave myself a stern talking to. *Right, my kids are now done. There's no excuse, Kate, step up! You've got your work sorted, now it's about time you look at yourself in the mirror.*

I hadn't physically looked at myself in the mirror for so long. I knew this was something I had to work on, and I was ready to get serious about it. The spotlight was now on my health, and there was no more room for excuses. I went to a personal trainer and tried different nutritional programs to get my food choices in order.

I had to learn that the core issue is that I am an emotional eater. So when I'm happy, I eat. When I'm sad, I eat. Even though I'd started my health kick, I used to secret-eat in a car park at McDonald's and not tell anyone. I would justify it with, "It's okay. I go to the gym." But I was undoing all of my good work with a single burger meal.

Exercise is never a chore for me. I enjoy it because it gave me space to have mental clarity and open my creativity to begin to envision new and wonderful things. I can really see clearly when I'm exercising, and I had been in a fog for years until that point. The endorphins that release through exercise make me even more motivated to want to look after my body. When I get to the gym four times a week, I feel proud, and I love myself.

I realised I had to align my mindset with my physical health goals so they could work in unison to get me where I wanted to go. I started working with a dietician, a hypnotherapist, and a food psychologist, and I also started to see healers, which rounded out a holistic approach to my health. I was screaming for help, and once I reached out for it, I put the bullshit excuses down and dug in. *Right, I've got to do this.* Once I set a goal for myself, I am all in. The business was running well, the team was in cruise control, and I felt like my health was the final piece of the puzzle, because everything external was beautiful.

I discovered that I love coconut water thanks to my friend Meera Allen. I drink a litre of it every day. I also drink less alcohol so I can have mental clarity to be able to perform at my best every day.

When you look at my overall business journey, 2021 and 2022 were the years of consolidation and "cruise control" in my business, and I believe that is because I was focused on my health. It just goes to show that you can never truly excel in all areas of life; there will be some that require more focus and energy at times than others.

I'm so okay with that, because as I write this book, I'm forty kilos lighter, and I have put the spotlight back on my business, because I am back in the driver's seat when it comes to my health and can put my health and food routine on cruise control to maintain it!

I go to the gym four times a week, which I do in the mornings before the school drop-off, and I make all my meals so I know they are healthy options. I started off going to a gym that was a fifteen-minute drive away from home, but now I've moved to one much closer. When you can find absolute convenience for exercise in your life, it is essential to keep you motivated and engaged. There is one non-negotiable treat I give myself: either an ice cream or a handful of gummy bears every night while I hang out with Jay after the kids go to bed. Yes, it is a "bad" ritual, but I'm okay with it, because I'm still a normal, functioning human being, and no one is perfect. My weight has not moved for nine months, so I have found my new normal.

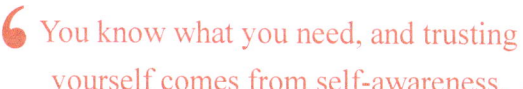

> You know what you need, and trusting yourself comes from self-awareness.

Understanding yourself is such a powerful thing, and it comes from being okay to stand up straight and look at yourself in the mirror, to own your past fuckups and be okay that you will likely make more. I know there are some people who are too scared to look in the mirror. They don't want to be self-reflective, because they just don't want to do the work. That's okay for them, but I'm not *così così*.

I know what I need for my mind, body, and spirit to function at my best. If I miss a few gym sessions because work has picked up or the kids need me, I feel it in my body. I'm so connected and aligned to myself that I can recognise and self-reflect really fast. There are times when I feel sluggish, and when I pause and reflect on why, it could be because I need more sleep or a Kate Day with zero plans.

Confession time! I like to sit up and binge on TV shows when everyone's sleeping. When there's a new season of *Survivor*, I will catch-up on the show and might stay up until 11 pm. I did that for a whole week once and was sluggish every single day. *I feel shit. I've got to do something about this!* Once I recognised that feeling, I forced myself to go to bed at 8.15 pm to catch up on sleep. I woke up with so much energy the next day and instantly felt better. It was all because of a conscious decision to break a habit that wasn't serving me.

By bringing my body, mind, and spirit into alignment, I am more in tune with myself than ever before.

Gold Nuggets for Health

There are some key ingredients to nurture your mind, body, and soul for holistic health. You've heard them all before, but sometimes, we need reminders!

They are:

- ⓢ Sun
- ⓢ Nutritious, healthy food
- ⓢ Plenty of water
- ⓢ Movement
- ⓢ Giving yourself space to recharge

So how does your commitment to your health stack up?

- ⓢ What are my non-negotiables when it comes to my health?
- ⓢ Do I eat the way I want to?
- ⓢ If I could change one thing in my diet, what would it be?
- ⓢ Can I create a new 21-day habit to improve an area of my health?
- ⓢ What am I doing to ensure my mind is taken care of?

- ⓢ When was the last time I spoke to someone about how I am feeling?
- ⓢ What type of exercise do I actually enjoy?
- ⓢ Where can I find more time for exercise?

CHAPTER 11
RESILIENCE

Between late 2021 and early 2022, KLCC went through what I can only describe as a Covid hangover. We had been partying for eighteen months, experiencing growth, and KLCC had become a million-dollar business. It was all roses, rainbows, butterflies, and unicorns.

As you'd know if you've ever experienced a hangover, they are not fun. Over November and December of 2021, we made $30,000... in six weeks. It was a huge drop from the dizzyingly high numbers we had been pulling in. While we had been immune to the "norm" of business – which was to struggle because of the ramifications of Covid – for so long, we had begun to fall into line with the environment around us.

There was a second wave of Covid that was scaring people. We went from single-digit cases in Queensland to over 10,000 in the space of a month. People were fatigued by mask mandates and by the uncertainty over what they could and couldn't do and who they could or couldn't see in order to follow public health orders as they shifted so frequently.

Businesses were shutting down, and people were being made redundant left, right, and centre. Job security was more important than ever before, and even people who hated their job or wanted to change careers were too scared to look at change. Any kind of movement seemed terrifying, because so much felt out of people's control.

Even in our peak growth phase, business slowed down over Christmas, because people prioritise other things over their careers at that time of year. It was standard for us to experience that lull every year, but Christmas of 2021 was brutal. KLCC was doing $14,000 months when it needed $25,000 to break even at the time.

This carried over into 2022. I view 2022 as the year of consolidation. We hit that plateau I had been anticipating (be careful what you wish for!). On the outside, it looked amazing. We turned over a million dollars easily, but the issue was that there wasn't much profit. The money wasn't coming in at the same rate, yet my overheads remained the same.

> **This proved to me that while growth is good, consistency is better.**

If we had more consistent months in terms of turnover, the profit would not have taken such a hit.

We hung on, and I kept hold of every single full- and part-time team member, which was my goal. We didn't go backwards, but we didn't go forwards, and that to me was a win. In business, you need to be okay with that, because some years are about maintaining what you have rather than continuing to grow. Let me tell you, though, that I was counting my lucky stars that I'd had the foresight to save up a $100,000 buffer when the going was good.

The year 2022 marked five years in business, and this was the chance to recalibrate. It is normal for most businesses to experience a plateau around the four- to five-year mark, so I used this time to get the people right, get the team training right, get the clients right... really just trying to get *everything* right in terms of systems, processes, and consistency.

Resilience is really key here. You have to sit in it, you have to feel it, and then you go into problem-solving mode. I knew that if I downsized my team, I would reduce our capacity to serve clients. After the crazy scramble of 2021, that was the last thing I wanted to sign up for!

Even after the business had its worst month, I didn't pull back. That's where I think differently to most. When people panic and stop spending, I actually scale it up, and this was particularly true when it came to marketing. Even though I saw the money literally pouring out of my business, I knew that I was able to keep going, and I was all in anyway.

If the calendars aren't full for the consultants, I will double down on marketing. It is the last place I pull money from, although it is the first for many. If there's a dip, I think, *let's hit it,* because I know advertising spend brings in revenue. If we go hard for a week, and there is no difference, I'll pull back a little, but never completely.

It's like putting on an extra consultant before I can comfortably pay for their wage. I know that by putting someone on, I will add to my payroll, but that $2,000 in pay each week gross could net the business $2,000 a day. So that's an investment that is going to pay for itself quickly. The reward doesn't need any explanation. But the risk? Well, is this the right person? How long will they need for training? Do they have the right experience? That last one was a tricky juggle for my career consultants; I tried hiring someone with coaching experience who had never worked in careers. Then tried someone who had careers experience but had never coached. You have to know when to pull the plug if someone is not working out.

I've been asked many times if I have ever thought about throwing in the towel or if I have ever had an experience while building my business that was terrible enough to make me think, *Hey, can I really get through this?* The honest answer is – of course I have! But being in business, being my own boss-has lit this fire in me that I don't think anything can dampen.

Of course, I try to be as logical as I can about it, and I always tell my clients to do the same.

> My golden piece of advice about keeping your business self-sustaining is to always prepare for famine while you are in feast.

Plan for the worst, hope for the best, and always keep reality in check. Don't be afraid to make the hard decisions early. There have been plenty of times when I made the decision to trim the fat before it was crunch time, but I learned this from the Covid-19 era where growth was happening at a faster pace than I could ever have anticipated. In that time, I was *reacting*.

When you react, you are automatically on the back foot, and that is where cracks can start to appear in your business. In your rush to implement, complete projects, employ, or whatever else you need to do in order to keep pace, there is no time to be deliberate and think things through thoroughly. In contrast, when you are *proactive*, you can pace yourself and consider all of your options before moving ahead.

Of course, no matter how proactive you are, occasions will arise where you have to react, and this is where your resilience comes into play.

I am staunchly loyal, and integrity means everything to me. In periods of famine within my business, I always make sure that my salary is the first thing to be trimmed rather than letting go of team members. I would much rather take a small cut to my income if that means I can keep the amazing team I have built. Keeping a beefy budget for the team and marketing is always my top priority. The first things I evaluate are my immediate overheads and my subscriptions. Those are the easiest things to trim.

Honestly, though, I cannot imagine a reality where my business doesn't exist. There is just too much demand, and when I see the impact I make every single day, I just don't think I could ever give it up. There is so much evidence that the business model I have created works and is sustainable. While there is one person that needs me, I will be open. I'm not interested in stopping. So I will continue to ride the ebbs and flows now until the day I die.

> In order to continue growing and continue being successful, change becomes a necessity.

It is powerful, even if it's bloody scary. In 2022, a huge change rippled through my business when my long-term right-hand lady and I decided to grow in our own directions. She was ready to spread her wings with more study, and I supported her decision. She had been a constant for me both in my personal and professional life for years. When this came up, I had to confront my own vulnerabilities.

There was no point in fighting the change. I couldn't selfishly ask her to stay with me because I was scared of what would happen without her. I had to be okay to let things be as they were, knowing there was something in there for me to learn. I had to trust there was a good reason why this was happening, and all would be revealed on the other side of that pain.

I had to trust the process... and trust myself.

I was alone at the helm of my business for the first time in three years, and I had to learn once more to stand on my own two feet. I'd done it before as a sole trader, but in 2022, there was so much more at stake. There was a team that relied on me to keep things moving so they could have a job to come to each and every day.

As I reevaluated how I had been working, I came to realise that I had become accustomed to working in a way that was dependant on another person. It wasn't the way I wanted to work. Thankfully, I had this wonderful opportunity to reinvent more positive working practices for myself.

I wanted to create a shift in my business life so that it stood completely separate from my personal life. I wanted to clearly define the roles, because I realised that I had worked so closely with her that the lines had become blurred. She was a friend, and naturally, work began to eat its way into my personal life. I wasn't getting the downtime that I needed, and my personal relationships suffered because of this as well.

I feel this happened because the bond we had was so strong. We got each other. We would encourage each other and constantly push one another to do more, achieve more. We were determined to be successful in business, and we were hustling for it. We were each other's biggest cheerleaders. We fuelled each other's passions for business and leaned on each other. We would even joke that we were each other's work wife.

Quickly, a routine developed where at the end of each day, we would call each other on the way home after being at the office all day. I so loved these after-work phone calls, because it was a time when we could chew the fat with one another. We could discuss the successes we were having, the challenges we were facing, or just simply brainstorm new initiatives and opportunities. Often, the drive home wouldn't be long enough, and our conversation would then become a Zoom call so we could continue talking business after hours. This became more and more frequent.

However, I came to realise that this change was an opportunity to evolve. This change really allowed me to grow. It allowed me to find my own momentum. Now, I am confident in myself and my decisions. I've become self-reflective and self-validating. I am totally empowered. This change allowed me to be rebirthed into the Kate Langford I am today, a powerhouse woman at the helm of a successful business.

Can you recognise a part of your journey that may have been tough at the time but ultimately built you into the awesome woman you are today?

My personal relationships have also shifted for the better and grown a lot stronger. I approach friendship in a totally different way now. Friendships should never become business and vice versa. I have found that while I can really value and have wonderful, positive relationships with people I work with, there really isn't any need for them to cross over to my personal life. Business is business, and friendship is friendship.

There have been times in the past when I was hyper-focused on business to the point that I really was neglecting my husband. Jay has always been my rock and my biggest supporter. I think I was just so caught up in trying to prove things to myself that I was unintentionally blocking him out.

I would come home from work and forget to kiss my husband hello because I automatically slipped into mum mode and made a beeline for the kids. Even then, there were nights when I had unfinished business conversations, which meant I didn't slip out of businesswoman mode at all even though I had walked through the front door. It took me a long time to realise how blurred the line had gotten between my business and my home.

Finding that balance and having the discipline to wear only one hat at a time is something I have definitely had to work at, but things are so different now. I share so much more of myself with Jay and keep the line between business and home clear. I've become much better at juggling all the balls. I now make deliberate time and space for all versions of myself, and my life is so much more fulfilled as a result.

I am forever grateful to Jay for his understanding during that shitty time when I wasn't learning the lesson I needed to. I love him for it so much. He saw the potential I had, the journey I needed to take, and let me go my hardest. I appreciate the selflessness that took on his behalf. We have grown together through it all. We make a wonderful team.

Both of us prioritise time together now. We focus on filling each other's tanks with the things that we know will make each other happy. I still make his smokos, and he has "me time" watching Netflix on the couch. He makes sure I get my me time too, and he'll put the kids to bed and arrange for a babysitter so he can take me out for a nice dinner. He'll take me on adventures and even take a pottery or art class with me. It all balances out, but you have to be willing to work for successful relationships, too, just like you would for a successful business.

With Lisa gone, I was back in hustle mode again. The business needed me, but I put another timeframe in place – this time six weeks – so I could hustle to my heart's content with a clear end in sight. I was back into the trenches again with the team so I could provide them with safety and stability after we lost someone who had become the second in charge.

Lisa wasn't the only one who moved on in 2022. KLCC went through a period of turnover of team members. My biggest challenge in business – and heck, maybe even in life – has always been hiring and managing my team. Team management is one hell of an emotional rollercoaster, even for someone like me who has been in recruiting for over fifteen years!

Hiring in particular can be extremely emotional if you let it. I've found that in order to be successful in managing a team, you need to have clear boundaries and a logical mindset. I think management of a team has always been my Achilles heel, because I have this deep, emotional desire to help people and see the good in them. Even when I used to be the boss of other people's companies, it was always something I struggled with. There have been times where I have hired the most amazing team but they have sensed my emotional weakness and turned on me. Now I have a golden rule that I present in each and every interview that I do. The rule is, if you take the piss, you're gone. Those are the words that literally come out of my mouth every time. I don't say it that way to be dramatic; it is simply a way for me to put the clear boundary in place without all of the emotional baggage that can come with it. It is always interesting to see how people react to that line, though. They either say, "Thank god, I've found home," or they tell me that I am scaring them and can't get out the door quick enough. Win-win.

As I was writing this book, I reflected on how there was a period of time in which I'd had very little success with replacing a career coaching position. I had burned through five different options who had either not accepted the job offer or who had started and not lasted for long.

Something is not right here. What is the common denominator? Oh, it's me!

It's not usually something people want to hear, but I'm really okay with saying it to myself *and* to my coaching clients. I've lost count of the number of times I've had to hold a mirror up for someone I was coaching. The conversation might go a little something like this:

"So, you have left four jobs in the last four years?"

"Yeah, the first boss was always looking over my shoulder, the second boss was super strict, the third boss was arrogant, and the fourth? Well, they were just annoying."

"That's interesting. So what do you think the common denominator is here?"

"What do you mean? Well, I just keep finding these bosses…"

"The common denominator is actually you."

"Oh… shit…"

I can be pretty blunt with my clients because they give me permission to say what needs to be said, but it can still be hard for some to hear, especially if it's for the first time. But you know what?

> It's *fantastic* news when we are the common denominator, because the one thing that we can fix in this world is ourselves!

If a common denominator ends up being me, I have to own it and then figure out how I can change how I do something in order to change the outcome that keeps repeating. As Albert Einstein said, "Insanity is doing the same thing over and over and expecting different results."

Okay, what is really going on here… I wrote down the responsibilities of the role, how it operates within the business, and what the salary is. Then I wrote down why all five people didn't last. One didn't accept because of the money on offer, one had a parent pass away, one wanted to homeschool their children, and two were employed and let go.

I reworked the parameters of the role and called back the candidate who declined due to the salary. I knew she was the most qualified for the role and upped the offer. She accepted.

Without that self-reflection, I could have run all kinds of fantastical stories in my head. *I'm not training people properly. I'm not communicating well. There's just no good staff out there. I've hit a wall and won't fill that bloody position.*

Instead, I can look at what is really coming up. What can I learn, say, or do to change things? How can I say I've done all I can to make the situation better? Once I am comfortable I have addressed all of those things, it usually leads to a very logical path forward to solving the issue.

Guess what? This process can work in any situation. That is my strategy in everything I do for everything from business to friendships. And you know what? Sometimes, I have already done all I can, and there's no further action I can take. On those occasions, I will be kind. *Kate, you nailed this. You did all you could.*

Just as Stephen Covey's Circles of Influence states, we have the power to change ourselves, we can influence the thoughts and behaviours of some people and outcomes of some situations, but the majority of the time, we have absolutely no control over what happens in life.

> The moment you realise you cannot change anything outside of yourself, it changes everything.

This all started to drop in for me in 2022. The team debacle that year had kept my hands full, but I honestly felt good about it. There was a sense of renewal, fresh energy, and more enthusiasm with every new person who came on board. With the energetic shift that occurred in 2022, the zing came back into the business. The team brought in $45,000 in just two weeks – and they weren't even *full* weeks due to public holidays. It felt incredible to be able to manage forty-five grand in eight working days. I knew it was because I was once again all in. You need to do that in business; otherwise, it'll eat you alive.

I felt like I could reset things and prepare us for another skyrocket. I didn't know when it would come, but I knew I wanted the team to be ready for whenever the rocket fuel ignited.

That's when I started to love myself more. I stopped chasing, I stopped pleasing, and I started to sit, be still, and be kinder to myself. I am the common denominator of patterns that keep recurring in my life, and as soon as I recognised that, I knew I had the power to change what wasn't working out for me.

Being anchored in myself with more certainty than ever, I truly felt like an independent businesswoman. I hadn't done much in the way of integrating myself into the business community up until then. At that point, I didn't truly know anyone in business on the Sunshine Coast because I had been so firmly entrenched in my own lane. I still remember attending my first dinner event and feeling so nervous because I didn't know anyone. I was worried about being out of place and not fitting in. I was asking myself, "Am I worthy of being here?" All those little insecurities and vulnerabilities we all have were running through my head. But I put my big girl panties on and went anyway, because I knew this was an opportunity that I needed to grab with both hands.

I quickly found I was a great networker, and I didn't shy away from going to events and meetings on my own. The Sunshine Coast Business Women's Network (SCBWN) helped me connect with so many like-minded people and has spawned so many other opportunities for me and my business. The risk of putting myself out there was certainly worth the reward.

I had another moment of imposter syndrome when I was approached to join the SCBWN Board. *Why do they want me? What could I bring to the table?* I realised that they could also see that I was levelling up. I said "Yes" to another opportunity and became the network development chair, in charge of onboarding new members into the network and being their voice in the boardroom. It felt so incredible to sit around the boardroom table with a collective of powerhouse women and, after a few meetings, I allowed myself to recognise that I *deserved* to be there.

Although it is rare that I don't accept an opportunity, there is never a one hundred percent success rate when you take on something new. There have been many times when I have run with an opportunity and tried my best to make it work but have ultimately had to make the call to call it quits on that direction.

> Being able to evaluate when to pull back or say no is one of the most underrated skills a businessperson can have.

For example, in 2021, I made the decision to engage with an enneagram personality profiling workshop. I saw that this personality profiling tool was trending massively online and was seeing a huge amount of engagement, particularly in the United States. I sought out a specialist here on the Sunshine Coast and decided to make the investment to run a workshop with them through my business. I paid for the marketing and resources. It was an investment of both my time and money. However, after about twenty hours of work, only one person had signed up for the workshop. The risk was not delivering the reward, so I made a call to pull the entire thing.

Having a successful business lifestyle is also about being resilient. It's about having the ability to pick yourself up and dust yourself off when an opportunity doesn't work out as planned. I'm a big believer in things happening for a reason.

> ❛ I understand that you can't always control the outcome, but you can always control your reaction. ❜

I could have been super negative about the time and money I lost, but that wouldn't have gotten me anywhere. Instead, I chose to sit and reflect on what had gone wrong. *Why wasn't interest sparked? Did there need to be a different approach to marketing this type of event? Had I simply backed the wrong horse?* Reflecting is another valuable tool any business person can have. It gives you a chance to change a perceived failure into a learning experience and to ensure the same mistakes are never made twice.

This is a difficult skill to perfect, because it means leaving your ego at the door. It's about being clinical. A successful businessperson needs to think logically and critically without emotion. Evaluation must be honest and cannot happen just to sooth one's ego, otherwise it is not an exercise worth undertaking. If you are stuck in making your ego feel better, you are going to sit firmly below the fucking line. The failure will be blamed on anyone and everyone, so how can you expect to be able to prevent it from happening again if you haven't taken responsibility for it in the first place?

Being successful in business means owning failure and learning from it so you can grow. You cannot be emotional about failure; otherwise, you will never be successful.

Gold Nuggets for Resilience

In April 2020, we were moving office again – the third time in three years. It was something I was pumped about, because the girls would have their own space for the first time. Everything was going well as we packed for the move. The removalist confirmed the night before they were turning up at 8 am on the Saturday, so I had organised babysitters and the works to make sure everything ran smoothly. The team had turned up and packed the cars with all the computers in the pouring down rain, only to find the removalist was late. We waited an hour and then called to find out they would not be showing up.

I had a million-dollar business that was literally pulled apart and no idea what to do. I sat there for a moment. People say to me, "How do you deal with things like that?"

I won't sit there and whinge about how bad it is. Instead, I'll sit there, I'll feel it, and I'll take the shock. Once that is processed, I go into action mode.

I rang Dad and Jay so they could come up and help pull everything apart ready to move. Then I remembered there was a removalist truck hire company that was a five-minute walk from our old office, so I set off to see if they could help us while the office furniture was being dismantled by the handymen. When I walked in, I requested a truck that would be covered in because we had to keep everything dry.

"You won't believe this, a truck was returned ten minutes ago that fits your description. That never happens on a Saturday!"

"I'll take it!"

Eighty dollars on the spot gave us the keys to the truck, and I felt so excited to be in the driver's seat of that thing that it could have easily been a new-release shiny red Ferrari! We got everything moved and set up in the new office before the day was through. It was absolutely exhausting, and I was bloody sore by the end of it, but we had completed our mission.

Too many people would have thrown their hands in the air the moment the removalist confirmed they would not show up. Resilience is really key here. How do you free your mind from stress and open it up to critical thinking in moments like that?

- ⓢ Sit in the thick of the situation – it's okay to acknowledge that things are shit for a moment.

- ⓢ Feel it – cry if you have to, punch a pillow if you must, but get all of the emotion out.

- ⓢ Get some rubber on the road – with the emotion processed, you can go into problem-solving mode *fast*.

When you can do this, nothing will beat you.

We all moved into the shiny new space on Monday morning, and I thought, "Wow, this is going to be an awesome day! We have fresh energy and have turned a new leaf for KLCC."

The first person in my office that morning was a casual who resigned effective immediately. She was an administrator, and my only other team member in that position was on holidays for a fortnight, so now we had literally no support for the inbox and incoming calls for a million-dollar business.

I went through the three steps, and by the time I reached problem-solving mode, I had been able to come up with a solution that was way better than the system I'd had in place prior to that resignation.

Resilience is knowing that there is always a reason things happen. When you can roll with the punches and understand that it won't always be sunshine and rainbows, you will be able to recognise the shit times for what they are and then switch into a mode that is productive and helps you to move forward. You need to do that in business, otherwise it'll eat you alive.

CHAPTER 12
LOVE

"My dear friend, Congratulations on your achievement of being a finalist this evening. I'm so proud of you stepping out and showing the world just how wonderful you are, not to mention the help and guidance you give your clients. As a friend your love and support is unwavering. I love watching you succeed. I see you and believe in you. Whatever the result tonight, you are a superstar."

This was the inscription inside the card handed to me by Paula Williamson when I attended the Sunshine Coast Business Women's Network (SCBWN) Gala Awards Night as a finalist in the corporate category. I was caught up in the whirlwind of the night, so I didn't get to read it properly until the following morning.

Although I didn't win my category, Paula's heartfelt message brought me to tears. I felt so fulfilled to have such a beautiful friend by my side. All I had ever wanted was to be seen, heard, and understood. They are basic human needs but ones I never truly had met by friendships as I was growing up.

For most of my life, I craved validation from anyone who would give it to me. I wanted boys to look at me so I felt beautiful. I wanted employers to tell me I was doing a good job. I wanted managers to announce I was the top salesperson at meetings so my peers would congratulate me. I wanted business awards to show the world that I was a great businesswoman. I wanted Jay to tell me that I was a good mother. I wanted so much from everyone outside of myself.

Guess what? It's tiring working hard to get the approval of other people. I don't need anyone else's validation any longer. I have reached the conclusion that love is really all you need; love of self, that is!

For sure, this realisation has come with maturity, experience, knockdowns and rebuilds, but it has been backed up with a decent serving of personal development and giving myself the space and time to *really* get to know myself. I also credit my kids for a lot of that maturity, too. My three kids give me unlimited validation. I have done the hard yards and know that I am okay within myself. I know I am working squarely in my genius zone, and the work my team and I do is making a difference.

It took me many years to experience true friendship. Even at school, I was in what was considered the "cool" group, but I was never really included like the other girls were. I was the nice one who supported everyone. I would listen to everyone's problems, help sort out the drama, and encourage others, but it never seemed to be reciprocated. I was forgotten about and cast aside a lot. I would get to school and feel totally on the outside, because the girls had been on the phone to one another overnight, and I had no idea what was going on because I was left out, or I would find out they had caught up to hang out the afternoon prior and I had been excluded.

Have you ever felt that?

In school, I was always just on the outside of the social circles I had. I was constantly taken advantage of. This seemed to be a pattern for a large section of my life. I've found in most of my friendships that I would care so much more than the other person, and it would always fall on me to be the one organising the coffee catch-ups, the girls brunches, and the birthday dinners and plans. I would always be the first one to send the "How are you?" messages and rarely received any in return. Friendship always seemed like a one-way street.

When I reflect on that time of my life – my teenage years, especially – I can see now that I was a follower. I never belonged with those people. But I forced myself to remain there. To try again and again to impress them, to get them to like me. I needed to be validated by the people I thought should like me just because I liked them. I struggled to know if these people liked me at all, and I would send myself crazy thinking about it. That uncertainty and not truly feeling anchored in a friendship was detrimental to the trust I had for others as well, since one of our core human needs is to feel like we belong. When I was left in that limbo state of "does she really like me, or is she just using me?" it was damaging for my mental health.

This pattern played out for decades. I hate to think about the number of hours I have wasted thinking about whether or not the people I hung out with actually liked me. The nights I'd lie awake analysing their behaviour and trying to evaluate if I meant anything to them or if our friendship was legitimate. The brain space I lost when I'd assess how many friends I had and from what section of my life they came from… Were they work friends? Family friends? Friends from netball? I would fixate on it because I wanted to make sure I had an "acceptable" number of friends in my life. Acceptable to whom? I don't fucking know. But I had told myself that the more friends someone had, the better a person they were. I wanted to be a good person – no, a *great* one. I wanted to be someone whom *everyone* liked.

After a lot of self-reflection, I realised that my low self-worth contributed to the way I approached and viewed friendship throughout my life. My low self-worth was the reason I accepted people using me and treating me like shit. I had been conditioned to surrender to everyone else because I was so conscious of pleasing them. I craved validation and would do all I could to receive confirmation that people liked me and were happy with me.

I realise now that most people never really understood me. How could they, when I was hiding my true self all the time? No matter how much I tried to express myself and my values, I was always misunderstood. Never seen. I was always trying my hardest to be loved and accepted, even though that meant I had to become a totally different person. I would have to hide and surrender my true self in order to become someone I thought they would like. Ironically, despite my efforts, I still didn't seem to fit in anyone's box. This led to me always feeling unworthy. I experienced this same pattern in my friendships over and over again.

It wasn't until I started honouring my true self that I was able to work towards breaking this pattern of behaviour. I stopped giving in to others and began to get comfortable in my own skin.

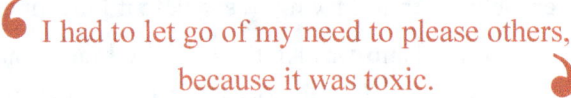

> I had to let go of my need to please others, because it was toxic.

It was keeping me down. There have been far too many times when I have been judged, disrespected, and patronised by other people, leading me to think that there was something wrong with me and that I was the problem.

When my self-worth was low, I accepted this behaviour. I saw it as normal. It has taken a lot of time and therapy to help me realise that kind of behaviour really *isn't* normal. There is absolutely nothing wrong with me or with the person I truly am. Gaining this knowledge and taking the steps towards healing has helped me reach a point now where I will no longer accept being treated like that. I know I am worth far more.

I have had to put in the work to get to this point. I've had to call myself out on the shit that I was allowing and accepting. I have had to look inward and be critical of myself. I've had to reevaluate my expectations of myself and others. I would always be going above and beyond, because the expectations I had of myself were always so high. I expected that everyone should have the same level of drive to be the best they can be and to be doing the most they possibly could, because that is the way my brain works.

I've come to realise that my super-speed brain is what makes me who I am. It is the thing that makes me great at what I do. However, it is unrealistic of me to expect that others think and act the way I do. I've had to learn to leave others where they are, particularly if they are operating from a place that is vastly different to me. I've really had to let go of what I cannot change and accept that while I am going a thousand miles an hour and others aren't. Instead, I choose to focus on accepting others for where they are and to not be afraid to step away if we do not align.

The same goes for the way I was forcing myself to act within friendships – to be the one running after everyone else. I refuse to do that anymore, because I refuse to engage in one-sided relationships. It means it's okay if I leave them where they are and choose to put some boundaries in place. I've come to realise that just because I will go out of my way for others does not mean others will automatically do the same for me.

I have had to consciously work on not hiding my true self just to make it easier for others to accept me. When you boil it down, bending myself into all sorts of shapes to fit someone else's idea of who I should be was a coping behaviour. It certainly wasn't one that served me! All it brought me was one-sided relationships. I have come to realise that I would never be accepted or truly seen by people who are not in alignment with my goals, so why should I be changing who I am? Why should I give up my aspirations just to make them happy?

Moving through this transformation of self was difficult. It took a lot of courage. I had to be critical about what and who I was attracting into my life. I really had to evaluate the part I played in whether or not I continued to foster relationships and friendships that were damaging to me. I had to have the balls to see people for who they really were. I had to find a real balance between shutting down to block out the toxic behaviour of others in order to protect myself and remaining open so I can evolve. All of this was some tough shit to work through. Ultimately, I have decided that I will never again shrink myself for anyone.

The more I work on myself, the more I realise that it isn't my job to surrender to others, to give up who I am just because it doesn't fit their mould. I've come to realise it is not my job to change the mindset or the behaviour of others. I am responsible only for how I show up in the world.

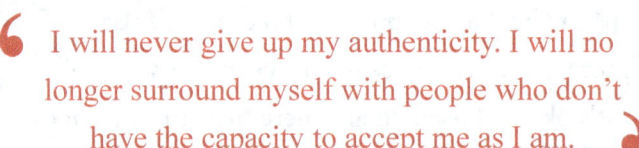

> I will never give up my authenticity. I will no longer surround myself with people who don't have the capacity to accept me as I am.

If you don't align with my vibe, morals and integrity, no problem, we are just different. That doesn't mean you are any less nor am I, we are just on different paths. The way you speak, seek to understand and hear what others think and feel while maintaining respect is key and through executing this in all areas, has really opened up to being with my kind of people.

I've stepped into my empowered era, and it is bloody terrific!

Learning to have reasonable expectations has been challenging, but it has helped me grow my self-worth. I have had to learn to be a lot less emotional and reactionary in my relationships. I've really had to evaluate what is personal and what isn't. I used to always feel so hurt when friends wouldn't extend the same level of support that I was giving them, because I took it so personally. In order to try to process the hurt I was feeling, I would enter into the never-ending loop of overanalysing and overthinking.

I put it down to the fact that I have a brain that loves to problem-solve, so overanalysing felt like I was running some kind of diagnostic testing on the situation to see what I was doing wrong. The problem with overanalysing is that the issue often grows legs of its own and can quickly spiral out of control. So I started asking myself this question: *Where is the evidence that this is true?* This is still an activity I use with clients all the time, too. Often, people who think in the way that entrepreneurs do are thinking and reacting at super speed. They have to, or they will never survive in the fast-paced business world. This means entrepreneurs and our amazing brains can create very elaborate stories very quickly. An anxious emotional state can sometimes be the place where our sharp thinking minds thrive, which can really be a curse. It is so important to stay in control of emotions and to practise slowing them down at the right times.

If I am ever in a situation with a friend, colleague, or acquaintance where I feel undervalued, or if a sense of tension creeps up and my head starts to run away with me, I always remind myself to run through the evidence test. For example, I might be entering that spiral of thinking things like *This person must not like me, I can't believe they are treating me like this or I must have done something.* My mind used to really like to paint me as the bad guy. That is when I have to remind myself to stop and ask, "Okay, Kate, where is the evidence?"

Most of the time, there isn't any. It's been a story that my head has made up during a bout of overthinking. If I trust and value the opinion of the other person involved, I can outright ask them! If I don't have that type of relationship with them, I can fall back on the evidence test, put the situation to rest, and move on.

If I find that there is some evidence to a situation – like maybe a colleague has shut me down a few times during a business meeting and is making me feel like they don't like me or don't value me – then I'm not afraid to have the tough conversations. I approach the person and, respectfully, clear the air. I present the evidence to the person, and I ask them what the issue is. This is the only way to squash overthinking and to be proactive in tough social situations.

I encourage my clients day in and day out to have those kinds of conversations when needed. I used to be so afraid of being assertive. I would shy away from having hard conversations because I perceived them as conflict. The reality is that tough conversations are a part of life. This has really helped me take the emotion out of situations that used to cripple me, and now it's normal to just get the conversation started. People who know me expect that of me, and some even love it about me!

Of course, I still have days where I doubt myself and fall into that trap of overthinking.

Understanding and learning to have better control over my emotions has helped me realise that, at times, my expectations and perceptions were warped. I was able to link the fact that some of the behaviours I was displaying, like overthinking, came from a place of wanting to be loved, accepted, and validated by others. Coming to this realisation was pivotal. It was confirmation that I wasn't crazy! Armed with this knowledge, I was able to learn how to change my approach to these behaviours. It has also made me aware of what triggers me emotionally.

Looking inward and being able to identify my own triggers has been game-changing for me. It has allowed me to understand my own emotions and reactions. It has also given me the freedom to think logically and critically about social situations rather than react from an emotional standpoint. This has given me a lot of power in social situations, where previously I would have been deeply affected by other people's behaviours and the way they treated me. Once triggered, it would be a hard and long road to recovery, because I didn't understand why these situations were making me feel as awful as they did.

Understanding my triggers and developing constructive strategies to process them has been valuable for business, too. I have been able to identify what provokes me negatively in my business life and devise positive coping skills to overcome them.

One of my biggest triggers was when I saw someone doing something similar to what I was creating. As a business owner, you become fiercely protective of your ideas and concepts. They are like your babies. Obviously, it was inevitable that other business coaches would move into the same circles as the ones I was in. There have been times when I have been face-to-face, literally, with other entrepreneurs who are using content very similar to the content I have produced. It can be really difficult to sit across the table from someone at a networking event and see them appropriating your content. This type of behaviour used to send me over the edge. I would feel the need to confront these people and call them out on their behaviour. If you know me at all, you would know that I am not afraid to call anyone out if I feel it needs to be done. However, when you are in the professional world and your brand is literally your first and last name, it isn't always appropriate. So I had to rein in going off half-cocked in order to not look like a crazy person and tarnish my brand.

I've worked hard to unpack what it is that triggers me about this. It isn't because I am threatened or intimidated. It's that I love what I do. I pour my heart and soul into my business. I work from my own unique genius zone. I work bloody hard to produce the highest quality outcomes I can. I truly value what I do and the clients I have so much. I think I used to get so triggered, because I would see others not putting in the same level of work as I was. They weren't tailoring the experience. This would really fire me up, as the client was not getting the same value or experience for their money. However, just like in my personal life, I have found ways to take the emotion out of it.

If I come across another business or career coach who is using content similar to mine now, I just remind myself to stay in my own lane. If they have to steal my work, then they clearly aren't operating out of their own genius zone. My motto now has become, "Stay in your own lane. No one else is Kate Langford." I have learned to have the confidence to sit back and watch it all play out. I know I can work through that triggered feeling without letting it spill out emotionally. I've learned how to keep myself on track and in a positive headspace.

Healing my reactionary behaviour has also helped me become a stronger leader and a more dynamic business owner. I'm glad I have found the confidence to be my true self, even if that comes across as a little blunt, as it is the way I survive in business.

Both in my personal life and my business life, learning how to take the emotion out of situations and become less reactionary has helped me level up. It has helped me feel confident in the person I am. It was only when I started working for myself and on myself that I realised how draining juggling my work and home personality was. I felt like I was always pandering to what my boss wanted from me. I did what I had done in my friendships in order to cope; I became this totally different person in order to please them and be the person they wanted me to be. It drained so much of my energy operating in this way. I remember always feeling so disconnected in my personal life. I would come home from work and still be wearing this fake mask I had put on in front of my boss. I found it very hard to let go of my work persona at the end of each day. It was like two completely different people trying to mesh together. The longer that identity struggle went on, the more angst I felt. I felt like I was slowly losing myself.

Working for myself allowed me the freedom to be my authentic self across all facets of my life. It liberated me. I could finally be Kate Langford. I could operate as her at all times. Home and work, it was all the same me. I am so grateful now that I don't have to try to keep up those appearances. Working for myself meant that my power, my strengths, my integrity, all of it was finally able to shine again.

I am tempted to say I transformed when I decided I'd had enough of working for someone else, but I feel it is more accurate to say that I emerged. Metamorphosed, if you will. This true self, the Kate Langford I am today, has always been there. She was just lost for a little while. Lost under the pressure to perform at work and keep a boss happy. Lost amongst teenage social angst of wanting to be liked and understood. Lost because she never had her place in the world, never had her people. But finally, here she was. Kate Langford emerged and everything started to fall into place.

I began to find my true friends when I shifted into the entrepreneurial world. It surprised me, actually, the speed at which I found my tribe as soon as I decided I was worthy enough to pursue my passion. I feel like there is a huge lesson in that.

> ❛ When you allow yourself authenticity, you will be rewarded with everything you have always dreamed of.

Entering the entrepreneurial world was scary at first. There were so many unknowns, and everything was so new to me. I wasn't sure if I would fit in. But I took to it quickly, mostly because of the people I was able to connect with. All my life, I have felt like a discarded puzzle piece that didn't fit or belong. However, when I started to attend networking events, this all started to change. I was finally mixing with people who shared the same sharp thinking skills. I was around people who had put in the work to become authentic versions of themselves. Being able to connect with like-minded people and build authentic friendships with them has been an invaluable experience. I was blown away at the ease of these friendships. For the first time, none of it felt like hard work.

It was only once I began to experience these true, authentic friendships that I realised how important it is to have people in your life who want to be there rather than people who feel they need to be there. This also goes for people you feel need to be there, too. If you have to fight to keep someone in your life, then it is worthwhile asking yourself if they really are someone who lights you up. Why are they someone you are so desperately attached to? Do they fill your tank? If the answer is no, then there is no harm in putting some distance there. The people you surround yourself with should value you, not drain you.

I've been blessed to find my true circle of friends, people who have shown me that friendship shouldn't be hard work. It should be natural and authentic and should build you up rather than tear you down. The friends I have now are honestly my lifeline. They are my blood. I feel so comfortable in their presence. Around them, I can be my true, authentic, and unapologetic self. They love me for me. They understand me. They share the same passions and match my drive. Experiencing true friendship and unwavering support, this has really helped me take things to the next level. Attending networking events and knowing that I am going to have these people there by my side has created a sense of calm confidence. I know I can tackle anything now.

One person who deserves an extra special mention is Paula, the beautiful friend of mine who wrote the heartfelt inscription to me at the beginning of this chapter. Paula is an angel, a true light in this world. She is as hard as a rock but is the most loyal person you will ever meet. She is one of the first people who ever really saw me for me. She is a very special person in my life and someone who I feel I will always be indebted to. Without her encouragement, acceptance, and belief, I'm not sure I would be where I am today.

Paula's friendship has allowed me to continue to build my self-worth and my confidence. If it wasn't for her, I never would have become the confident and outgoing person I am. I probably never would have been involved in all of the amazing opportunities she has helped connect me with. One such opportunity was to connect in with the SCBWN. In 2021, I was nominated by SCBWN president Roz White to enter the corporate category of the SCBWN Awards.

I had another moment of believing I wasn't good enough when she called to tell me about the nomination. I still didn't see myself as being in the same calibre as past winners, despite already having won national Ausmumpreneur and Roar awards the year before. Do you find that your mind plays tricks on you like that at times? I was already a national award winner and I was worried about putting myself forward for a regional award! It seems pretty silly when I write it in black and white, but the truth is that I was comparing myself against past winners, some of whom had gone on to win major awards like the Telstra Businesswoman of the Year, and I didn't think I would make the cut. All of that changed when I spoke with Roz, who said, "Kate, you need to go for these awards."

"But I feel so selfish doing it. It's not all about me."

"And that's exactly why you should be going for it!"

I didn't really understand at the time what she meant, so I went to chat with Paula, and she said, "Kate, if you can't make this about you, then think about the amount of people that you can help more by getting these awards and nominating yourself."

As soon as that was said, the penny dropped. *Well, if I can help more people by winning the award, then I am all in*. That was my drive. From then on, I couldn't put it down. I had to work on these awards. I thought about it night and day. How to sell myself wasn't exactly easy, although I help people sell themselves all the time.

But then, I remembered that it wasn't about being loved by others; it was about being recognised for doing my job and running a bloody good business. I think you should acknowledge when you have done something well.

 It's time we lost the shame in saying, "I'm doing well!"

It's not arrogance to accept you are awesome at something.

I made it into the finalist shortlist after filling out a huge application form. I made it through a panel interview and got all dressed up to stand on stage at the gala awards night in September. It was overwhelming, and I was buzzing with anticipation to see if I had made the cut or not. Paula and many of the women I was now able to call friends were coming up to congratulate me on being a finalist throughout the night.

Finally, the moment came when my category was called out. I lined up to the side of the stage, waiting for my name to be called as my cue to head up the stairs. In a pre-event meeting, we had been instructed to walk to the centre of the stage to collect our finalist certificate, shake hands with the award category sponsor, smile for the camera, and exit on the other side of the stage. We then went into "The Purple Room," where all of the category finalists congregated to wait for the announcement.

"And the winner is..." *Not me.*

The competitive driver in me was disappointed, but for the first time ever, I was able to brush that to the side almost instantaneously. I knew I had felt extreme pride as I stood on the stage moments earlier as the event MCs read out a list of my achievements. To me, that was the moment when I felt like I had truly earned my stripes. The fact that I didn't walk away with a trophy that night did not bring me down. I was evolving.

I had entered the Sunshine Coast Business Awards, and during the finalist interview, I walked in, the technology didn't work, and I could have lost it out of frustration. Instead, I stood there, and I was just me. I stood in my power, stood in my zone, and showed what I'd achieved with KLCC and how much I loved it. I just became so grounded in who I am and really owned my worth. I think that came from standing on stage at the SCBWN awards night.

Later that year, I was invited to attend the 2021 Pyjama Summit. The summit is a not-for-profit retreat held in Buderim on the Sunshine Coast where businesswomen could connect, share, and support one another. The 2021 Pyjama Summit was held in April, and at the time, I was really starting to step into my power. I'd put in all of this hard groundwork in self-development and was finally at a place where I had confidence in myself, my values, and my beliefs. As part of the summit, I was asked to take the microphone by Roz White, who is the company director of White's IGA Group. I decided that I would speak about my journey, particularly about shedding friendships and about personal growth.

Taking the stage at the summit was a huge moment of vulnerability. I remember standing there in my pyjamas and thinking, "Am I really about to pour my heart out?" But as I looked around the room, I knew that I was surrounded by like-minded people who had my back. I knew I was surrounded by people who saw me and understood me. I knew I was supported. This knowledge gave me the confidence and courage to speak my truth.

I used the opportunity to share my inner thoughts about the power of friendship and the importance of finding your own tribe. I opened up about my own struggles with friendship, about giving so much to others and getting hurt. I let myself be vulnerable and shared how difficult it had been for me to find people who accepted me because of how my brain was wired. How I found I would always butt heads with managers that I worked for or be told that I was too intense or too emotional. I spoke about how I had always thought there was something wrong with me and how this changed when I moved into the entrepreneurial world and began operating out of my genius zone. I encouraged others to shed the friendships or business relationships that no longer served them.

> I gave them the advice I wish I had received – be authentic and don't hold on to what other people want you to be; rather, move into who you truly are.

The summit really was a lightbulb moment for me. After speaking, I was flooded with support and had so many other entrepreneurial women approach me and express that they'd had similar experiences. They, too, had felt like everyone was trying to box them in or condition them to be anything other than who they really are.

So many women feel judged, unaccepted, and unseen throughout their lives. Some even confided in me about times they had given in to altering their personality in order to be liked or valued. Being open and honest about these experiences allowed others to feel safe enough to share what they had been through. I feel like the Pyjama Summit was a place of healing for so many of us, and I am grateful that I could help facilitate that openness.

I was overwhelmed to be thanked and praised by so many inspiring women for sharing my vulnerability and my truth. It really touched me and solidified the importance of sharing my experiences. Hearing those words of affirmation from others was pivotal for my self-love and confidence, too. My experience at the Pyjama Summit left me feeling empowered and stronger than ever before.

The confidence that has been built through healing my mindset in regard to friendships and social interactions has been phenomenal. I am a firm believer in the idea that the hard work you do on yourself rewards you ten times as much as the hard work you try to put into others. I am in a wonderful place with the small circle of people I call friends. And you know what? I think that is how I know I've made it. The awards and accolades are nothing compared to knowing I have found my place in this world. To know I am surrounded by people who see me for who I am. Because that was the one thing that I never, ever thought would happen for me. I never felt worthy enough of finding my tribe, but when I let my true self shine, my tribe found me. It's one of the things I am most proud of, actually. Making money, feeling loved, being recognised, all of that is great, but understanding I am worth all of those things is what makes me so proud.

Gold Nuggets for Love

Relationships are a foundation of life. When you look at the core loves of our lives, we have love of self, romantic love, love as a parent, and love as a friend. One of my key learnings towards navigating all of those forms of love was getting a grip on my mind.

It's so easy to make assumptions and to let our minds run away with all these made-up stories that seek to justify our assumption to make us right. Guess what? All it does is send you batshit crazy and block you from opening yourself up to any form of true love. It's not the most fulfilling way to live.

The best ways I have found to get a grip on my mind is to:

ⓢ Know your triggers.
Take note of when you fly off the handle with rage or break down into tears. What is the underlying cause of that reaction?

Is it a story you find you tell yourself over and over again with different circumstances?

ⓢ Determine if the story is real.
Get real about what is happening. Write down the *facts* that you know to be true about the situation that has triggered you. Facts include what was actually said, what was actually done, and how it played out. Facts do not include why you *think* something was said or why you *think* someone was

"motivated" to behave a certain way. Leave all unknowns off the table.

Once you have all the facts, you have effectively removed emotion from the equation.

Does the story still ring true?

⑤ Choose your course of action.
We always have a choice!

If the story is untrue, it's time to dedicate space and energy to unpacking that so you can be emotionally free of the shit that is clogging up your mind and causing you unnecessary breakdowns.

If the story is true, pick a course of action that serves your highest purpose. It could be letting go of a friendship or an employee, or working with them through conflict resolution to strengthen your connection to avoid future blow-ups.

The power of choice is always there.

CHAPTER 13
BALANCE

Balance is the golden goose of life, isn't it? If you tame that bugger, you can claim that you have "work-life balance," and you are set, right?

Let me start by explaining what I believe balance is; it is *not* being perfectly spread out amongst all of your commitments. It is about having the presence of mind to be able to know what you need to prioritise at any given time. It is knowing yourself well enough that you have developed your own sense of values and boundaries and you are confident in your ability to stick to them.

> 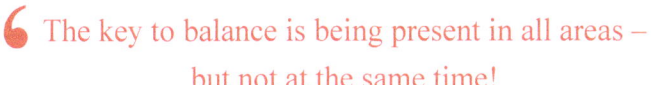 The key to balance is being present in all areas – but not at the same time!

Just a reminder for you that balance has never meant *perfection* in all areas; anyone who sets out to have that as a life goal will likely fall flat on their faces.

When you are at work, be present at the office. When you are with your family, be anchored in whatever activity you are doing together. You do not want to be mentally preparing a presentation for Monday when you are in the middle of a family board game on a Sunday afternoon. The fact of the matter is, you'll end up doing a crap job at both activities; your presentation will suck, and you will likely end up losing the board game because you aren't giving either your full attention.

161

As you know, I was about six months into starting KLCC when I found my balance was out of whack. I was disconnected from my family. I could hear them laughing in other rooms of the house and having fun together while I was working after hours in my office. I *hated* that feeling, because I was working in order to spend more time with my kids, but there I was, being taken away from my kids because of work.

I was able to recognise the problem early on and rectify it by hiring my first team member. I could have told myself I wasn't ready to take on the financial commitment of a team member and keep working myself into the ground, allowing the disconnect with my kids to last longer. There are so many who do. But I was like a lioness with my cubs, and there was nothing – not even my business – that could come between me and my babies.

When I am in hustle mode, I get stuck in and get shit done. It's not the time for "I'll just…" No! I get in and get everything done. Because I know that once I have, I can return back to some sense of normality in my routine.

I have had to break hustle mode before. Life happens, and when I am receiving cues from my kids that they need me, all bets are off. They might start to get clingy, more emotional, or perhaps have quite big reactions to small things, because they are feeling heightened. I pay attention to those things, because it means they are not feeling safe and settled, which are so important for me to provide as a parent.

Discipline is a huge component of balance. When I see those cues in my children, I have a choice to make; push through and ignore their needs, or remember why I am in business and dial back so I can ensure they are okay. After all, kids are only young once. Whether it was feedback from school or day care that they weren't coping, or realising that my interactions with Jay had boiled down to simple kisses hello or goodbye, they were all indicators I paid attention to. If there was a sign that my home life was out of balance, I would take action.

I had to check myself, too. I am an emotional eater, so if I notice I am eating a lot more bad food, or if I am tired all the time, I look at my routine and see where I am falling off the wagon. I have also caught myself saying, "Oh, I just have to do this..." when one of the kids has asked me to do something with them. The moment those words come out of my mouth, I know that my compass is askew. It means that I believe *everything* is important at work and not just my responsibilities. It means that I have slipped back into control mode, and that's a problem. It's a problem for my team, because I'm stepping into their roles unnecessarily, and it's a problem for my family, because I am stepping into my work hat far too much and not being present at home.

Of course, work is important, but if I start prioritising it over all else, then I have actually already been taken over by the evil, greedy work gods. Their sole purpose is to keep you always locked into a work mindset. *No! I'm in control here!* Recognising that work is actually controlling you is the first step towards being able to shift and move your attention and focus across to the things you value most. As you saw in the Growth chapter, I'm huge on being proactive rather than reactive. If I can be aware of those subtle changes in the way myself and the people around me behave, I can change my schedule, because I am in control of it. I see too many people with their heads down who end up disconnected from the people who love them the most because they surrender to the greedy work gods and don't even recognise it. By the time they understand they are prisoners to their career or their business, it might be too late to react.

Being proactive means having presence in everything you do. When you are present, the person, activity, or task has your full, undivided attention. Business and career women wear so many hats; career slayer, boss babe, sexy wife, nurturing mother, sister, daughter, personal chef, cheerful cleaner, punctual Uber®, sport cheerleader, limitless imaginative play partner, schedule keeper, team builder... on and on it goes.

There is no way you could balance so many hats and excel in every single one of them *all* of the time. To think that you can, or *should*, puts you on the express train to Burnoutville. Believe me, I've seen it countless times in the people I work with. They have tried to perform all of their roles to perfection, and it is not only unsustainable but unattainable. The quicker you realise that, the more in flow your life will be, and the less shit you will put yourself through.

Presence is simple, really. When you are doing something, you are not thinking about the list of things you have to do before you go to sleep that night. You are not thinking about the conversation with a boss that didn't go so well the day before. You do not have your hat backwards or forwards; it has to be on properly so it is comfortable. When you have your hat firmly on your head, you are in the moment. You can feel, taste, see, hear, and smell everything.

When you take that hat off and exchange it for the next, you then move into presence for that role or task. Then, as the hour grows late and it's time for sleep, you slip on the night cap and dedicate hours to rest – not scrolling through your phone while tucked in bed!

Presence works for me because I live on the extreme of whatever I am doing. I don't want to be mediocre, or *così così*. I don't want to be half-arsed with anything I do. If I'm playing Matchbox cars with the kids, I'm commentating the race and making the engine noises as they zoom around the track. If I'm with a client, I am one hundred percent locked into the words they are saying and their body language so I can cut through their BS and get straight to the point so they can fly in their career or business.

> Give presence a try. It'll change your life.

It wasn't until after Lincoln was a few years old that I started to realise my Kate hat was being neglected. I'm talking about the hat I've had with me my whole life, not the ones I have collected along the way that define the roles I play. Let's be real, guilt is a palpable thing for working mums, and the thought of being away from your family to have time for *you* can be a confronting thing to entertain.

Well, I didn't just entertain the idea. Like all things in life, I've gone all in. In 2022, I established Kate Day. One day a week is all mine to do whatever I choose to. I think it's healthy because it gives me a chance to recharge my batteries. Kate Day is when I am fully present with myself.

First of all, I believe having boundaries with your children and putting yourself first actually teaches them resilience for the real world. I think if you constantly worry about pleasing your kids, what actually happens is you stifle their ability to grow emotionally. Kids are resilient, kids are strong, and kids need to know it's not all about them. That's just my parenting style, anyway, and I acknowledge that's not always for everyone. Long before Kate Day, Jay and I would have date night, and the kids would know when those were scheduled because we wrote them up on the calendar in advance. It was a cool thing to teach our kids, because when they grow up, they will know that giving to their partner is important. Plus, when the kids leave home, it's just going to be me and their dad, so we'd better have a bloody good connection!

I say it all the time: I am a better mother when I have had a break. Before Kate Day, there were times when I would react to something small by going from zero to one hundred in a flash, or I would start sleeping in and taking shortcuts as a parent. I knew then I needed a timeout, but they were few and far between.

I know if I clicked my fingers, my life would be over, so I want to have memories. I want to stop and smell the roses. I want to have massages and think about how I am feeling. I want to stop for me so that I can actually enjoy life. Because this life isn't all about my kids or my business; my life is about me. Being a parent is one of my roles, but it's not my *only* role.

I had a wrestle with mum guilt, but I took that bitch down ten pegs so I could create Kate Day. I had to think of it logically; in my immediate circle, I've got my needs, I've got Jay and his needs, and I have the kids and their needs, and that's literally how I visualise it. If too much time is going into one, the other two suffer, and if no time is going into one, the other two suffer. I can't be the best mum and wife if I am always of service and don't have any presence in my own hat.

To be completely honest, Kate Day was actually born out of frustration. I had reached a point where I was serving everyone else, and I had lost myself in the process. I woke up one morning and thought, *That's it!* I went to the movies by myself, sat there with popcorn, and allowed myself a chance to breathe and escape into another world. When the lights came on at the end, I didn't rush back to the office or home. I went and got myself a massage. When I did return home, I cringed as I turned on my laptop to see what kind of damage I had left in my wake by have the day off.

Guess what? Nothing blew up. Nothing imploded. Nothing even remotely urgent had come up that my team couldn't handle without me. *That wasn't hard!*

Having a non-negotiable weekly Kate Day has been the best thing I could have done for myself, my family, and my business, because when I come back, I am one hundred percent present. I look forward to Kate

Day, because the moments when I am in it, it feels bloody great, and I feel very deserving and worthy. The chance to stop and reward myself keeps me going and boosts my gratitude, especially when there has been a rough week. Because I am all systems go throughout the week, Kate Day also gives me a chance to step back and look at the bigger picture and get my creative juices flowing again. If there is something brewing, I can let it marinate on Kate Day without the need for immediate action.

I have a rule that I only book one thing in for Kate Day each week, and I let the rest unfold as it needs to. I might book in for a sauna or a massage, and once I'm done, I'll see what my energy level is like. If it's high, I'll call a friend and see if they want to catch up. If it's low, I might go to the beach by myself or head home to couch potato with some Netflix. I might even – *gasp!* – have a nap! Some Kate Days, I have loose plans, others I have none, but no matter what happens, there is a cardinal rule – it must fill my tank.

Ever since consistent Kate Days came into my world, my kids have been happier, I have felt more fulfilled, Jay gets more of me ☺, and the business has been flourishing.

Gold Nuggets for Balance

What's the point in building your own business if you can't find some sense of balance? By balance, you know my definition is really being able to dedicate time and energy to the areas of your life that lift you up.

My typical week looks something like this:

Monday, Tuesday, Thursday – work nine to five.

Wednesday – Lincoln day. We do swimming lessons, we read books together, and I have a sleep when he goes down for a nap.

Friday – Kate Day. Friday night is footy with the kids and sometimes fish and chips for dinner at the beach.

Saturday – Fun family stuff, birthday parties, and other events.

Sunday – Sacred family-only day. We shut everything down and get into our pyjamas at 4 pm ready to watch the Sunday afternoon footy with a platter of nibbles.

Grab your journal and give yourself some space to think about the following:

- ⓢ Do you feel like you are able to be present in every moment?

- ⓢ If not, what do you think stops you from doing that?

- ⓢ Can you commit to a mindfulness practice when you feel your brain moving into overload mode?

- ⓢ How can you build more balance into your routine so you can nurture your passions as well as your work?

- ⓢ What do you do just for you?

- ⓢ If you could do something just for you, what would it be?

- ⓢ If you created your own version of Kate Day, what would you call it? When would you have it? What would you do during the day to fill your tank?

- ⓢ If you cannot spare a whole day, when can you carve out half a day or even a few hours?

CHAPTER 14
VISION

"The next item... a four-night stay at the luxurious Eden Health Retreat in the stunning Currumbin Valley! Bids starting at one thousand dollars!"

I raised my hand. It was a no-brainer. A chance to spend a beautiful week with some girlfriends and escape for a while. I was dressed to the nines and having an incredible time at the 2022 Steps Winter Ball. The black tie annual gala is the major fundraiser for the Steps charity, which aims to give every young adult with a disability or autism the independent life they deserve.

"Do I hear fifteen hundred?"

Another hand in a sea of four hundred shot up.

Damn it! I've got competition!

"Two thousand?"

My hand went into the air. Backwards and forwards the bidding went. I was determined to win, and you know what I'm like when that competitive streak comes out!

The increments were getting smaller, up $200 at a time, and then $150.

"Do I hear four thousand dollars?" the energetic auctioneer called out.

I shot my hand into the air.

"Four thousand dollars, how about four thousand one hundred and fifty?" he asked, directing the question to the man on the other side of the room who I had been in an all-consuming war for the past few minutes. He shook his head.

YES!

"Four thousand dollars going once... going twice... sold!"

"Woohoo!" I jumped out of my seat. I started mentally writing the invitations to my besties as the volunteer walked over to my table to collect my information and take payment.

"So, how many people is the prize for?"

"It's for one person."

Shit! I screamed in my head as I handed my credit card over, my girls' week vision disappeared in an instant. I instantly felt guilty. *How am I going to take a whole week out for myself?* Little did I know, the power of giving yourself permission to remove yourself from the routine of everyday life to sit back, breathe, reflect, and look forward – it was exactly what I needed at the time.

I already felt like I was in a great place. In terms of my energy, 2022 was a year I spent really working on myself, and I thought it had really paid off. I came out of that year flying. It is the best I had ever felt about all aspects of my life. It's not like it was a walk in the park, though. There were plenty of challenges. I moved my business to a bigger office space, all the while going through the lowest month of revenue since I started. I was recruiting left, right, and centre, dealing with challenges in my personal life, and putting in the hard yards working on myself and taking accountability for everything I could improve about myself.

I've reflected a lot on this period of time and come to the conclusion that my mindset is what carried me through the ups and down of that year. I was locked in and manifesting that 2022 would be a growth year for me and my business. I wasn't giving myself any option other than to transform myself and my business. So I would ride the waves. I would face each challenge, give myself time to digest it, and settle into the new rhythm, and then it was onto the next thing. My belief system had changed. I knew I could deal with whatever hand I was dealt, so I just kept going.

Having a vision is one of the driving forces of success. Even if you are the world's greatest "doer," how can you ever have it all if you don't have a goal to achieve or a vision to reach for? If I sit back and look at my life, there have been many personal goals I have achieved: found the love of my life, had my three children, and have the white picket fence (literally – Jay and I put it up in 2019!) Professionally, I have a million-dollar business and have built a solid core team to run KLCC while I pursue my next passion project (all will be revealed in the next chapter...)

I create a vision, and then I go and get it.

There is no limit to what that vision can be, either. The missing piece that finally fell into place for me in 2023 is the importance of having a vision for *yourself*. I had been driven my whole life to have a vision for what I wanted to achieve on the sporting field or professionally, but I had not spent nearly enough time on the vision I have for myself as a person.

The beauty of a personal vision is that it doesn't have to fit into standard rules or even have a time limit in which to achieve it if you don't want it to. But the one thing it *does* need is work. You can manifest opportunities, but if you don't do the work when they arrive on your doorstep, then what was the point?

My professional goal when I started this business in 2018 was to reach a $10 million turnover in ten years. That means I have $5.8 million to go (next five years) at the time of writing this book. Is it possible? Hell yes! I am going for 15!! Will it happen if I sit on my arse and just hope the universe delivers it to me on a silver platter? Hell no!

I have worked my arse off to have it all. It has taken focus on my emotions, physicality, mental health, and sense of self to get to where I am. It hasn't just turned up; I've worked for everything I have. It infuriates me when people say I am lucky. Sorry, but I don't believe in luck. You *create* opportunities and maximise them.

 Having it all comes down to your vision and how you execute it.

Your ability to have it all is determined by your belief in yourself, your commitment, your desire to put in the effort, to do the work, and to make your own luck, to find your own balance, all of those sorts of things.

People who want to have it all but don't do the hard work to create their own luck won't ever get there. They will be stuck in the land of the "gonnas," where so many people are anchored by their own shit, because they are not brave enough to face it head-on.

It sounds cliche, but it really is all a choice how much you want to make your life awesome. You can wear all the hats if you want to. Not only that, but you can do it well if that is your vision, because then you will find a way. If you are busy telling yourself that it's too hard, you will crumble at the first hurdle. Why? Because you either have not developed resilience, or you simply don't have the patience to understand that success in *anything* does not happen overnight. In either case, you will need to prepare yourself to have that long, hard look in the mirror. I know it's scary, believe me, but if you aren't prepared to do the hard yards, well, your vision is never going to come to fruition.

If you let any or all of those things beat you, it's not bad luck; you only have yourself to blame.

The first business vision I had was to create Above and Beyond Resumes, and it worked because it allowed me to work around my family and also focused on writing résumés, which I knew would directly help my clients. Armed with a professionally-written résumés, they could boost their confidence to apply for jobs they would have been a little scared to pitch for previously. That lit me up and gave me all the fuel I needed to keep that business running, even when I had my two little ones *and* a part-time job as well.

I had run off the power of being in my genius zone since then, but I knew there was something new and exciting on the horizon. I knew there was something that I still needed to solidify in myself – that personal vision – in order for me to take that next step with complete commitment. The thing is, to have a vision you are passionate about, you need to give yourself the space to actually process what that is.

I don't mean a weekly Kate Day; I'm talking about a solid chunk of time – like five nights away! This is how you can truly disconnect from everyday commitments and engage with yourself on a deeper level. I have no doubt it was not an accident that I misheard the auctioneer at the Steps Ball and bid on the retreat. I never would have raised my hand if I knew the investment would be just for me. In a way, it was the universe having my back, knowing the timeout was exactly what I needed even if I couldn't see it for myself.

I felt all the mother's guilt around as I went off to indulge in a five-star luxury retreat on my own. I actually waited until it was about a month off expiring before I booked the damn thing in and committed to going. I packed a fresh journal to write in, because I just knew it was going to be a powerful week. So, when I went on that personal getaway to Eden Health Retreat in 2023, I set the intention to create personal visions for my future and work on strengthening who I am as a person.

I arrived at Eden on 5 March. I was absolutely blown away by the beautiful surroundings, having driven through the winding roads of the Currumbin Valley with a mountain on one side and beautiful, lush forest on the other. It felt like another world. Everything was absolutely pristine, luxurious, and high class in the main entrance, just enough to make me feel a little underdressed in my activewear. I lugged my suitcase in. The team was absolutely divine, and the moment I entered into my gorgeous villa, I flopped onto the bed and let out the biggest sigh. *This will do nicely!*

I was nervous, excited, and scared all at the same time. Nervous because there was *zero* mobile reception and I would be forced into a tech detox while I was there. Excited because Eden was breathtaking in every possible way. Scared because although I'd had time out before, I had never truly put all my hats down for five days in a row.

Who am I if I don't wear a hat? Will I like what I see when I put down all of the hats? Do I love myself enough to simply be myself?

On day one, these were the thoughts that were buzzing around in my head. I was worried someone would need me. *What will happen if they can't reach me?* The next moment, I felt pure bliss and was congratulating myself for taking the time out. It was a real see-saw, and I was getting nauseous from the constant up and down.

On day two, I woke up at 6.20 am and accidentally found a pocket of service after I threw my phone onto the pillow as I got ready to have a shower. It started buzzing with incoming emails and social media notifications. Hello... I lay on my stomach on the bed and reached out to swipe through the messages, careful not to lose this golden position.

I spent five minutes responding to emails before I realised what I was doing. *Stop it, Kate! This is not why you are here!* I remembered I was there to honour myself with this precious time and turned the phone off. The word I had chosen for myself at the start of 2023 was "Stillness."

When a word resonates with me, I find it incredibly powerful. I feel it in my body. It's as if there is a connection that gives me an intuitional hit, and I instantly feel its relevance to me. I choose a word that represents an overall feeling or state I want to achieve for a year.

The Eden Retreat was my first opportunity to put stillness to the test. Every part of my body wanted to do all the things, activities, walks, but my challenge – and I knew this – was to sit still. I want to be comfortable with boredom. I didn't want to talk for the sake of talking or scroll for the sake of scrolling. I just wanted to *be*.

I had a restful day with the most delicious organic food and very few activities and went to bed that night feeling like my batteries were finally on their way up to being fully charged for the first time... well... *ever!*

On day three, I went to a group awakening session. It was a chance to try something new with an open mind amongst a group of men and women I had never met before. The facilitator took us through a few exercises, asking us to tap into memories from our past that may have defined who we are today. During that session, I decided there were stories that needed to go. I no longer wanted to carry any part of the past that held me back, so I released everything that felt heavy and repetitive.

Then something else came up; I could not truly experience stillness and slow down my lightning-fast mind if I did not spend more time in feminine energy. I needed to trust and feel safe. I realised I was so strong, controlling, and fierce in my business and in my personal life because I did not truly feel safe emotionally. I was still protecting myself from that hurt in my younger years. I knew Jay made me feel physically safe, but I was still not open to allowing him to support me emotionally so I could fall down, cry, and be vulnerable. I was still in warrior mode, even within my own marriage. I know that's not Jay's fault. The exercise showed me that I need to know I am safe inside for myself. He can then step into his masculine and be there for me because I allow him to.

On the third day, I woke up at 6 am knowing that I was about to conquer a fear. Ever since my near-death skydiving incident, I haven't exactly been a fan of heights. That morning, I knew I wanted to smash it out of the park (in true Kate style) so I could free myself from another mental barrier. Eden has a flying fox that runs through the forest, and I signed up to go on it. Might sound simple, but man, were my palms sweaty, even just standing on the platform. I announced to the retreat staff that I wanted to go first so I didn't have too much time to dwell on it. One of the staff did a safety check of my harness.

Shit, shit, shit!

"Kate, you're up!" I was so tempted to turn around and run back to the safety of my villa, but I took one shaky step forward. I locked my goal into place. I was going to step off that ledge come hell or high water. My hands were shaking as I grasped the handle and the team secured my safety harness to the cable. When I took that step off the security of the ledge and threw my trust in the harness to get me to the other end, I could have lost it... but I didn't.

Remember how I wanted so badly to feel that rush of adrenaline and all-consuming high when I'd skydived but I didn't? Well, it hit me with full force on that flying fox. I was smashing the fear out of this world and out of my life, and boy did it feel bloody amazing!

I booked an abdominal healing, manifestation, and sound healing for the afternoon. There was a pool of emotion that felt like it was growing larger by the hour within me. All day, I had felt like I wanted to cry, but I couldn't. I wanted to let go, but there was something stopping me. While I was in my abdominal healing session, the healer said I was all in my head.

I felt offended by that comment, because I had always thought of myself as an intuitive person. But what I realised is that I was so set on having it all that I lost flow somewhere along the line and became a tick-list person of achievement. *For whom? For what approval? The old wounds of survival are still in my life. Can I finally feel safe?*

After the healing session, I went to the villa for a nap. When I woke up, I ran a bath and sat in there, trying to clear my head and sink back into myself. I looked at my naked body in the tub. Like, really looked at it in admiration and respect. *Whoa! You did it, Kate. You gave birth to three kids. You've lost weight. You've got a successful business. You've been married twice. You have built strong friendships and are overcoming traumas. I did all of it, thanks to this body.* It was this moment that I realised I was so disconnected from my body, and I needed to bring it back into alignment with my mind. I felt like I was truly seeing my body for the first time in a decade. I'm back. *I see you. I value you.*

 I felt an overwhelming sense of gratitude in that moment of connection and acceptance, of my whole self.

The final day of my retreat was 8 March – International Women's Day! I wanted to give my body the chance to be heard after I had been in my head for so long. As I sat by the pool, I felt peace, open, alive, and truly connected. I wrote down a list of ten items that make up my personal vision:

1. Reconnect with my body. I am one with it. I am thankful for it and grateful for all it has done for me in my life.

2. Balance the nervous system, hang out more, rest, and know you are safe.
3. Body movement. While I am all about pumping weights to build muscle, balance that with moving my eyes, hips, and legs for feminine energy.
4. Let go of stories I am hanging on to from the past.
5. Be softer with Jay so I can sink into my feminine and allow him to step into his masculine energy.
6. Manifest more.
7. Surrender.
8. Know I am safe with my mind, body, and soul when they are one.
9. Language is key; work on communication.
10. Overcome any fears with determination.

It's funny how the universe likes to test your resolve once you set down a new vision for yourself. Surrender, soften, and move into feminine flow were some of the key takeaways from my retreat, and within two weeks of returning home, my first real test came: my personal assistant resigned. As you know, when unexpected team member changes had happened in the past, I would be sent into an emotional spin. But this time around, I was in such a state of flow and trust that this did not ruffle my feathers at all.

I was happy for her, because she was moving into a field that she was passionate about; her genius zone. I moved the team around a little, and it was barely a blip. Having successfully navigated an event that normally would have triggered me, I was rewarded by the universe with two opportunities to present: one as a panellist speaker, and another at a careers conference at the University of Western Sydney.

I felt like I was levelling up in all areas as a result of the clarity of this personal vision. I looked different. I felt different. I was slower but still sharp. My team commented that the pace of my voice had slowed right down and became measured in how I spoke. It was like I no longer had to operate at a million miles an hour, which had been the standard pace for me my entire life. It felt nice. It's like flexing a muscle that has always been there but seeing the results from remembering it and using it! Business is like that too!

Setting business goals was something I had always been comfortable doing, but now I felt much more centred in my ability to set personal visions for how I want to show up in the world and be a better human.

Gold Nuggets for Vision

Life gets full! Without presence and balance in your world, you can put your head down to work, and when you lift it, years have passed. When was the last time you dedicated space to looking at your personal vision?

- ⓢ Create some space in your calendar now to check out of everyday life and spend time defining your personal vision.

- ⓢ Are there barriers to you taking that time? Talk to your support network to find solutions.

- ⓢ If no opportunities exist, allow them to come. They will show up in unexpected ways!

- ⓢ Challenge yourself by completely unplugging during this time away.

When you get the space to focus on your personal vision, consider:

- ⓢ Do I have a vision board?
- ⓢ What goes on there?
- ⓢ How am I showing up?

- ⓢ What do I want to change to allow me to be more in flow in life?
- ⓢ What stories am I hanging onto from the past?
- ⓢ How can I let them go?
- ⓢ Are there long-held fears that are holding me back?
- ⓢ How can I let them go?
- ⓢ What are the top ten personal vision outcomes I want to manifest?

CHAPTER 15
GUIDANCE

While it's true I have drive, passion, and determination for days, there is only so far you can get on your own before you hit a ceiling.

I hit my first ceiling early in business, and that's what led to me borrowing $5,000 to attend the retreat in Adelaide. My second ceiling arrived when I was in my second year of business. I decided to trawl through the global market and found a business coach from the USA who was great, but she was a little bit "woo woo" for me. Instead of giving instruction, she would constantly ask, "Well Kate, what do you think?" It frustrated me, because I was there for strategy, not mindset. I was overcoming imposter syndrome on a daily basis in those days, so I had that shit under control. I only stayed with her for six months, but she was absolutely brilliant at sales, so I learned a lot from her in that realm. That was a USD 10,000 investment.

It sounds like a lot, but I have a simple test; if it makes me scared, then it's a good thing for me to take the leap. If I know in my gut that the investment required is ridiculous, then it's not the right thing for me in that moment. I will always put it through the risk-versus-reward filter, and if I can manage the financial commitment and the excitement is even slightly greater than my fear, I will do it. I actually teach people how to navigate this in my sessions, because I've been through it so many time, and I get it!

I was pushing back during the first few sessions with the US coach as she wanted to move the structure from underneath my feet, which was literally like taking the heart out of your body. My whole business, my whole being, was made around structure, especially having three kids and a business to manage. Her request that I *change all* of that up was just too much for me.

I remember that first week I worked with her, I was absolutely exhausted. I hadn't slept because I was being tested on every level, and I was nervous about handing over so much money to something that I couldn't see the value in. I remember thinking, "Gosh, the money I've paid her, I could buy two jet skis."

The problem here was that I had not determined that she was right for me; I just jumped right on in and expected she would be a good fit. So handing over money to someone who said they don't do email, they don't do structure, was an absolutely groundbreaking moment for me. But at the time, I trusted the process. I had to go all in, and so I did.

I decided to promote Lisa to COO as per the US coach's instructions, because what I needed to do was to start handing over the little things like tinkering on Facebook and flicking between screens when I was sitting in the office my two days a week. I needed to start becoming creative again. In only the second or third meeting, my coach made me realise that she wasn't going to give me direct instructions to make the change I needed. I had to work it out for myself with her guidance, and this was a revelation for me, because I was out searching for someone to tell me what to do so I could just go ahead and do it.

Well, little did I know that this coach would challenge me on every level. I wanted to work on the KLCC business and make sure everything was ticked and crossed and done right and scaled as much as it could. She said, "Well, I don't want to do that, Kate. That's boring."

"But I need it."

"No, that's not the way forward. You don't need me."

"What do you mean?"

"You know how to do it. You've just got to do the work. You wouldn't be successful if you didn't know what to do."

This was the epiphany moment where I realised I had to get back into my business and really get creative and get right in there.

Within the next week, I'd written out profits. I'd written out my offers and what I was making on each of them. I'd organised a business planning day with Lisa coming up with new programs so that KLCC could literally start running itself. I also hired two people within a week. So being the doer that I am, I literally realised, "Okay, let's get KLCC sorted. I know how to do it, and if I don't know, I'll find out how." This is when things really started to move for me.

 I believe every coach needs a coach.

After three years of operating without one, I felt it was time for me to seek another one out in 2022. I was connected through my dear friend with an incredibly successful businessman who was giving his time as a mentor. I was chomping at the bit for him to cast his eyes over my business. I wanted to know if there were any holes that I needed to fill in order to bust through that ceiling. I couldn't for the life of me work out what the hell was holding me there.

I met him for the first time in August 2022. He asked me why I was in business, and I shared with him my desire to have a business that would allow me to have it all and also help every single one of the people who connects with the business to establish themselves in a dream career or to build a business that keeps them in the genius zone.

After a two-hour meeting, he leaned back in his leather chair and had his feet on his desk.

"Kate, you pleasantly surprised me. I thought Frances was sending me one of her friends just to help you out, but I can't find any leaky holes in your business…"

Wait, what?

"Every person who comes through this door, I find them instantly. You do not have any. You are ready. The way ahead is to scale."

"Yeah, I've thought about getting a general manager on board. Maybe in six months?"

"No, you've got to do that now."

Shit!

I knew he was right. I knew the next step was to let go of KLCC.

I had already said "Yes" to an opportunity that came out of nowhere – the chance to create Kate Langford Business Consulting (KLBC). I am constantly in awe of where my business journey has taken me. It all started when I connected with an acquaintance who approached me expressing a desire to start their own recruitment agency. They had no idea on how to get it off the ground, and I remember thinking, "I have the experience to coach you through this." And truly, that is where it all started. That is how my first client came to be. This one landed right on my plate and gave me an opportunity to move back into that creative, big-picture space where I truly thrive.

She asked me for help, and I knew that I could deliver! Up until that point, I'd had numerous people ask me to share how I had navigated one part or another of my business journey, and when I told them, they were blown away. Just like when I'd shared my marketing plan at the Adelaide retreat and everyone was in awe, I thought it was weird, because it was something that just naturally came into my mind. When the woman became my first KLBC client, I knew I could tap into the fast-thinking problem-solving brain I had to help others build their own million-dollar businesses. The thoughts that came naturally to me did not drop in so easily for others. My desire to help women succeed had taken on a whole new dynamic! I could continue to nurture people to feel confident to pursue the career of their dreams and could now help those entrepreneurially-minded women to bust out and build their own empires!

I mapped the steps that I took from the moment I decided to leave my previous job to where I had arrived now at having established KLBC with KLCC already being a business that had a steady seven-figure turnover. The result was seeing six clear steps that I took to get from A to B. These six steps became the building blocks of what KLBC would offer. I expanded upon these six points to flesh out each into sessions I could offer my clients. I created courses that became the foundation of the service I offer my clients. My business evolved organically through this reflective practice.

I started small and took every opportunity I could to grow KLBC. It began with consulting one-on-one with business owners and charging an hourly rate. My client base was building slowly but surely. I had so many people asking me what I had done to grow my business, and this is when I began to look inward at my own journey. I realised that the path I had created for myself was unique and that I had a true skill for building business.

It truly did unearth itself, and I will always be grateful for that. The opportunity to launch into KLBC came at the perfect time. I wasn't feeling as excited or passionate as I had about KLCC anymore, now that the majority of the hard work had been done. The vision, energy, and building had taken place, and it was running like a well-oiled machine.

> I quickly realised that creating something from nothing is my genius zone.

Being able to problem-solve and think outside the box to make shit happen is where I feel alive. Because KLCC was operating so well without me, I felt weighed down with all the ins and outs of running the business. The joy had gone for me. I realised that, as much as I loved working in careers, my passion did not lie in operations.

I knew KLBC could really scale, and I needed another challenge. I needed to break free of the groundhog day I felt like I was trapped in. It didn't mean I no longer wanted to help people find the career of their dreams; I was just done with managing the people who were doing that under the KLCC banner very successfully.

One of the things that was really powerful about that meeting was that this mentor recognised how much of my heart was in my business. "You know, Kate, one of the things that will help you go a long way is that you haven't talked about zeros once since you've been in here. You have talked about your family, you have talked about being able to help people and have it all, and that's why you will be successful."

He saw me and how clear my belief system is. Let's be real, as much as I rely on myself to be my biggest cheerleader these days, everyone needs validation to some degree, and to get it from someone who had done business much better than me felt incredible. Once he confirmed my thoughts that a general manager was the next step, I went all in, and the next week, I had a job ad up.

This mentor helped me to realise that I am a born entrepreneur, not an operations manager. I knew I would have to forfeit around $80,000 a year to install a general manager so I could free myself up to put my entrepreneur hat back on. In a true test of my fortitude, at the same time I was having these discussions with my mentor and weighing up paying the wage of a general manager, KLCC lost $30,000 in revenue over two months, and the bank account was the lowest it had been for ages.

Just as I knew hiring a career consultant for $2,000 gross a week would potentially get me $2,000 a day in sales, I understood that an $85,000 to $90,000 investment was opening me up to an unlimited potential to stretch my legs and see what I could bring in through KLBC. I knew being in my genius zone again would propel the business forward into another growth phase.

I back everything I do, and I don't regret bringing on a team member, as I know it's not serving me and my family, my headspace, or my burnout to continue to push through without that support. You need to know when to shift, and if you don't, you will crumble very quickly.

It was a turbulent time. I felt like I was dragging my feet, like I needed a complete change. I even thought about walking away from KLCC altogether, but I knew I didn't want to give up everything I had worked so hard to create. I also knew that I just couldn't go back to working some corporate job. I didn't want to be someone else's employee.

So I made the decision to hire a general manager to take over the operations side of the business. At the time, this felt scary. There were a lot of uncertainties. I only had five consistent KLBC clients on the books at that point, but I just knew deep down that this was a risk I needed to take.

Boy oh boy, did it pay off! Hiring a general manager allowed me to step into the role I had always dreamed of having. It gave me freedom to have some distance from the operations side of my business. I could be the person actively building the business of my dreams, delivering the services that my clients wanted, and KLBC would be given everything it needed to thrive. I started to feel that passion again. I could focus on business-building strategies. I could focus on creating the best outcomes for my clients. I get to help my clients build their businesses, and that fills me with so much joy.

Guess what? My general manager didn't last. I had worked myself to the point where I felt comfortable letting KLCC go, handing over the baby in September 2022, but it wasn't meant to be. In early 2023, she asked to step down into a part-time consultant role due to health reasons.

Holy shit! It's all over! I let my emotions hold a little too much power over me at that point. It took a no-bullshit catch-up with Roz to snap me out of it.

"Roll your sleeves up, just get back into the business, and do what needs to be done."

Of course. I'd done it before when Lisa left, so why does this need to be any different? That advice gave me the rocket that I needed.

When things like this happen, you have to surrender. Dreams are important and help to keep you creating and in flow, but they don't always unfold the way you hope they will. There is a reason why my GM didn't work out, but I wasn't yet ready to see it. I pushed and pushed and tried to find a new person to step into the role. That carrot of being able to step back and focus solely on KLBC was such a big one, but I could feel it being pulled further and further away from me.

I began to stress about how I could put it all back on track, but then one of my mentors said to me, "Kate, why are you trying to push shit uphill?"

She was right. When you release control and stop forcing things to happen a specific way, magic happens. That sound advice is one of countless pieces I have had delivered to me thanks to the mentors and coaches I have worked with to get me to where I am.

I spent a good couple of months in limbo, wondering what it was that I was missing but no longer trying to control the situation. KLCC was back on track and making good money. I shifted the responsibilities of my PA so she could help me more, but I still had that high frustration of not being challenged. There was a lack of excitement around KLCC.

I was stuck at that $1.2 million ceiling, and while I had a small group of trusted mentors, I knew I needed to find another business coach with strategies to grow the profit margin and scale. I had a choice to make: do I remain at that level and be okay with it, or was I ready to level up and start playing big again?

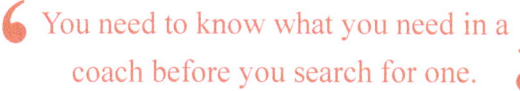

> You need to know what you need in a coach before you search for one.

I knew with absolute certainty I needed someone to get me from $1.2 million a year to $3–5 million without having to work 24/7 because I wanted to remain true to my core value of family. That was when an international award-winning business coach came into my world. I knew I needed someone who was really blunt and was going to give me what I need without the BS.

I was locked on to them because they knew their stuff, and I called their office to ask for an appointment to see if we were a good match. "No, sorry, they doesn't take one-on-ones anymore." I wasn't taking no for an answer, so the receptionist put me through to their personal assistant, and I had a chat with her. After about fifteen minutes, I said, "To be really honest, I only want to deal with this coach directly."

"They don't take one-on-one clients anymore, but I will speak to them about you. They need to see you. They are going to love you, so let me see what I can do."

Later that same day, I got a call. "You have Monday night at eight o'clock. Spend an hour with them, and you can find out if you are a fit and if this can work in group coaching."

"Great! Let's do it!"

I went into the first meeting with a potential business coach in 2023 knowing what I needed from them and pumped myself up for a high-powered conversation. I did not sit down in their waiting room; I walked around, paying attention to the framed awards hanging on the walls.

Alright, I'm not here to be pitched to; I'm here to qualify you. Are you really good enough for me? You need to impress me.

By the time I was called into his office, I was nervous but so incredibly ready. *I'm in control here.* I had flipped the script in my head, and it felt incredible. When I sat down, I leaned over with my elbows on my knees and clasped my hands in front of me – a classic masculine pose – and said, "Alright, what have you got?"

The smile that spread across their face let me know I'd set the tone, and they were ready to go.

They told me they had meetings since 6.15 that morning and I was their last for the day at 8 pm.

"Oh, so you have no energy left for me then?" I teased.

"I'm an engine!" came their bold reply. We had a powerful conversation, and they wrote all over their whiteboard as we spoke. They quizzed me on my processes and the numbers KLCC was pulling in.

"And what is your budget?"

"I don't have budgets. I just know my numbers and limits (obviously working, I thought)."

"Strategy?"

"It's all in my head."

"Right. Let's get real. You have a very consistent business that is kicking serious goals, you have the gusto and business-savvy mind that comes naturally, but you are lacking in your strategy and finance."

"Yes! This is my problem!"

I felt fired up, and I knew it was coming to the point when we would talk dollars. "Alright, give it to me straight. I'm not here to fuck spiders!" I demanded.

They picked up three folders and slid them across the table.

Here comes the pitch! I wasn't intimidated. I was ready. *You know what? I'm here to make change in this world. I know where I am going. I can see the vision. I just need someone to teach me what I don't know.*

The coach walked me through the first folder – a big group of people who meet regularly for full-day coaching sessions.

"Everyone I have seen today is going into this."

"Okay, cool…"

"You would froth over what I teach you in the first session, but you would be fucken frustrated in five minutes beyond that."

Ah, yes! This is the juice that I need…

They then pointed to the second folder – group coaching.

"Here we have smaller groups around the table once a month. I'm not going to lie; I have no space in any of those groups. I might have some in sixty days or sixty months, but right now, I have nothing."

Surely, the last option is…

"What's the third one, then?"

They sighed. "Kate… I don't take one-on-one anymore. I don't advertise. But you need that. You need me in this room for ninety minutes every four weeks. That's where you need to be."

I was beaming.

"Okay, I will deal with the fallout, but I am happy to take you on in that."

"Don't bullshit me. Have I got something good here?"

"Honestly, Kate, you need a lot of help with your financials and your vision and all that, but you are savvy as hell. With your marketing and your high turnover without those things in place, there are not many people like you."

"Yeah, I'm pretty ready."

"We are one-percenters in the world, you and I."

"You're keeping up with me?" I quipped.

"Hey, you are speaking my language. I get everything you're saying. I'm on the same page as you are, and your story is the same as mine. I'm literally looking at myself, and I know you are a business coach too, and I want to teach you it all, because I'm about abundance, I'm not about scarcity." Boom, so am I!

"Okay. How much are ya?"

When the figure dropped, I was faced with another risk-versus-reward moment... and that combination of excitement and terror that I knew came every time I was on the edge of something great. Now, this coach turns over millions. They did not need me to come on board. What was a holy crap figure for me was play money for them.

So I knew that I had a big decision to make. I reached out to trusted mentors, including Roz White, and she asked, "What's the cost of staying where you are?"

It was the best line that I could have got. Of the five people I spoke to, one cautioned me against it, but I knew in my gut that this was the right direction. I was just scared of the investment... See the word there?

Coaching is not a cost, it's an investment.

I rang their office to clarify a few small points and then went into logical thinking mode. I set myself a goal to bring in the money I needed each month to cover my coaching. I know myself well enough to know that if I am driven and set myself a challenge, I will get it. I felt the excitement pulsing through me – just like it had when I was writing up all of my résumé clients onto my new office whiteboard in the very early days of KLCC. My genius zone was back!

Okay, how am I going to do this? Well, I would have paid a GM anyway, so let's just pretend that my coach is my external strategist to assist in that role.

It was while looking at this goal that I realised why my general manager had stepped down! Without her exiting that role in favour of part-time work, I would not have looked for a new business coach and found my powerhouse coach. *Oh, universe, you sneaky bugger!* It got me even more pumped that I was back in flow and trusted that I would be able to bring in the clients I needed to cover my investment for coaching.

When you feel like you are pushing shit up a hill, it's actually the wrong hill! I am now much more aware of that energy and recognise that when something is just too hard, there's a reason for that. I had pushed for four months with no real outcome, but I hadn't been paying attention to why.

Want to know the best thing about trusting the process once you have set a goal? In *two weeks*, I signed up six new KLBC clients.

Six.

I created a chart that covered the twelve-month commitment to coaching, and the months were already being crossed off! What the hell, right? The universe delivered. I knew I was charting a course for scale even bigger than the one I powered through during Covid, and this growth was going to be sustainable because I had a master of scale as my coach.

I was nervous and scared but also clear, focused, and excited. I felt so in flow and back in my power.

I am at a place in my life where I know what my purpose is. I know the people I'm serving and the ways I can help them. All my choices had led me to that point where I could be working in a capacity that lights me up and fulfils me. I can attract people to work with me who are honest and want to be challenged. They are not afraid to look in the mirror and be prepared to make the changes they need to. They are prepared for me to tell it to them like it is but give them the tools that they need to go forth and smash it.

I have taken control of my own destiny in order to reach this point in my life. I have made a business lifestyle a reality. I love the job I have created for myself and the way it allows me the freedom to have a life outside of work. I have never felt more liberated in my career. I have found a way to have it all.

Yes! I can have my cake and eat it too. Bring it on!

Gold Nuggets for Guidance

You need to know what you need in a coach before you search for one. That was something I learned early on with the "woo woo" coach who definitely wasn't the right fit for me. If you don't know what you need, you are wasting your money.

In my early days in business, I fell into marketing messaging and was swept up in what I thought I needed, because the ads told me I needed it. If I had taken the time to know what I needed, I could have made targeted progress much sooner. Let my lesson be your guide!

Grab out your journal and consider these questions:

- ⓢ What stage am I at in business? Do I need someone to help me set up, to consolidate, or to grow?

- ⓢ What areas of my business do I know I need support with?

- ⓢ Where have I been struggling?

- ⓢ Where do I lack clarity?

- ⓢ Do I want black-and-white strategy, mindset support, or both?

- ⓢ What do I want my coach to have accomplished? Do they need to have achieved the type of success I want for myself?

- ⓢ What type of personality do I learn best from? Someone who is soft and nurturing, or someone who cuts through the bullshit and tells it like it is?

- ⓢ How much am I prepared to invest? (What is a no-brainer number, what is borderline scary, and what is way out of my league?)

Don't forget that you have the power to qualify your coach before you sign up to anything, so don't be afraid to put them through their paces to pitch to you!

ABOUT THE AUTHOR

Kate Langford is living proof that, as a woman, you can have your cake and eat it too. She has grown her business from a garage start-up to a million-dollar company, all while raising her three children and maintaining her social life. Not only is she passionate about encouraging people to find the job they love, she also wants to empower and educate other women on how they can find this balance.

So often, women are told they need to make sacrifices to either chase a career or family life – Kate is determined to change that outdated mindset and show women why and how they can have it all.

After over fifteen years working in the recruitment and HR industries around Australia and becoming certified in HR, business management, and counselling, Kate came to a point in her life that she felt like she had more to give.

She designed Kate Langford Career Consulting to help the people who really need it, and she continues to impact lives with her award-winning straight-shooter and real-life approach.

Being a mother to three children under eight, owning and directing a million-dollar business that has tripled (through Covid and while having her third baby) in five short years has been a huge achievement she is immensely proud of, all while helping change the lives of people across the country.

Kate Langford Career Consulting is recognised as one of the top career coaching companies in Australia, transforming lives from toxic

About the Author

work environments, feeling underappreciated, being underpaid, lacking career growth opportunities, or just not loving the job to creating roles that are designed specifically for career seekers and their lifestyle.

Kate now has a graduate certificate in career development and is a member of the CDAA. She launched Kate Langford Business Consulting in 2023 to empower people to fire their boss and create the business of their dreams.

Kate is a professional member of the Australian Centre for Career Education and the Career Development Association Australia.

Awards and Accolades

- Roar Awards Silver Award Winner 2020
- Ausmumprenur Silver Award Winner in Business Excellence 2020
- Ausmumprenur Silver Award Winner in Rising Star 2021
- Ausmumprenur Bronze Award Winner in Service Business 2021
- Stevie Awards Winner in Female Entrepreneur of the Year 2021
- Sunshine Coast Business Women's Network Corporate Business Woman of the Year 2021 finalist.
- Sunshine Coast Business Awards Education and Training 2022 finalist
- Featured in *Women Inspired, My Weekly Preview, Shine Business Women* and *Sunshine Coast Daily*

Kate is available for podcast and media interviews as well as speaking engagements and is an expert on the following topics:

- Finding your purpose in your career.
- Doing a job you love, not one you know.

- 💲 Women can have it all.
- 💲 Finding the balance in business and home life as a woman, wife, and mother of three young children.
- 💲 Kate's story of how she built a business from herself to fifteen staff Australia-wide and seven figures in three years.
- 💲 Teamwork and the importance to create success as an owner.
- 💲 Business mentoring.
- 💲 Mindset.
- 💲 Culture in business.
- 💲 Automation and funnels.
- 💲 Résumés, interviews, job searching, and career confidence.
- 💲 Any other topic required within the business or career coaching space.

Or to work directly with Kate and her team, find more information on the KLCC and KLBC pages to follow.
www.katelangford.com.au

KATE LANGFORD CAREER CONSULTING

Kate Langford Career Consulting (KLCC) assists people to identify their dream role – using a holistic approach – and then guiding them to land the role through resume writing, job-searching strategies, career/confidence/interview coaching, and many programs/memberships/packages that help hundreds of people every week.

Recognised as one of the top career coaching companies in Australia, KLCC transforms the lives of people throughout Australia and New Zealand through their honest and authentic approach, transforming lives from toxic work environments, feeling underappreciated, being underpaid, lacking career growth opportunities, or just not loving the job to creating roles that are designed specifically for career seekers and their lifestyle.

We offer a wide range of career packages to fit your needs! Everything from holistic career coaching to résumés, selection criteria to job-searching skills, career confidence and interview skills; we've got you covered!

Why do we do this?

After fifteen years in recruitment and HR, Kate saw a huge gap in the way career support was provided for individuals. The old "tick and flick" process for helping people find a job role just didn't cut it.

Kate found that so many career coaching businesses use this approach, so we decided to work with the person in a holistic way, through working with WHO they are and not just what is in the résumé.

We believe that you should do what you love, not just what you are good at. That's why you won't find career coaching or résumés like this anywhere else!

Jump on a FREE twenty-minute career strategy call with us to see if we are the right fit for you and what package might be suited. (No obligations, we are here to help).

Book here: https://www.katelangford.com.au/book-appointment
Get in touch: ask@katelangford.com.au

Praise for Kate Langford Career Consulting

"For twelve years, I never thought I was good enough to do something else because of my own ideals of working in an office. My whole entire thought processes about work, my life, how I feel about myself, and how much I have actually got to give to a great company have changed."

– Aimee Jayne

"The short videos are full of positive information that are direct and meaningful. They are easy to digest and easy to follow. I work full-time and study but still found time for this and it helped my study, plus it helped me find my passion and keep me on track! They perfected my résumé, cover letter and LinkedIn profile. If you are looking for career support, Kate Langford's program is so professional and l highly recommend it."

– Gary Smith

"Kate offers practical and professional advice on what you deserve in your career.

The steps are useful and actionable. In my opinion, don't sit back and wait for change to come to you. Get after it today!!"

– Dafydd Williams

KATE LANGFORD BUSINESS CONSULTING

Know you want to be your own boss but no idea where to start? Scared you need savings to start a business?
Frustrated with not knowing what to do as a business?
Treading water at your workplace and hitting a brick wall?
Unsure how to tackle marketing?
Good at what you do but not business-savvy?
Feeling like you've lost your confidence?
Want to know how to get paid more doing what you love?
Want to know how to use Facebook and Instagram marketing?
Think you don't have experience or credibility?
Not good at sales?

Kate Langford Business Consulting offers business coaching for high-flying employees to start their own businesses and become an employer without losing money!

Refine your business concept, niche your audience for ideal clients, and plan your next steps with a trusted professional who has been there before.

With over fifteen years in recruitment, management, and HR positions around Australia, and becoming qualified in business management, HR, and counselling, Kate came to a point in her life where she felt she had more to give.

After being recognised for fast growth within her own million-dollar business, Kate Langford Career Consulting, matched with a refreshing straight-shooter and authentic approach, Kate has gone on to win several awards and found her passion for helping others bring their idea to life.

This is where KLBC was born – to help you sack your boss, achieve the same results, build the ULTIMATE and profitable lifestyle business, and bring your passion/idea to life!

Be YOUR OWN Boss and do it confidently from the word GO!

www.katelangford.com.au/business-services

Book here:
Get in touch: ask@katelangford.com.au

Praise for Kate Langford Business Consulting

"Kate was the person I needed to help give me the courage to re-launch my Life Coaching Business. Sometimes it's not what you know, it's working with someone who believes in you more than you do yourself to get you back in the game. I am forever thankful to Kate and am so incredibly excited to be working from home again in my own business on my own terms. Thank you, Kate Langford."

– Lynn Levitt

"The business side was not my strong point and I didn't have the confidence to put myself out there, as an expert in the field. Kate's mentorship has made all the difference and my dreams and those of my family are becoming closer thanks to coaching with Kate, she's a legend! Coaching is an easy sell as it saves you TIME! You're paid back super quickly, it's a no brainer."

– Troy Smith

"Kate has been 100% the best decision I have made this year. She has helped crystallise my dream life doing what I know will make a difference. Her advice is always spot on and her X factor is how quickly she gets to the core of who you are and what your strengths are. She knows how to motivate and guide you in the best possible direction for success. I think Kate will be a part of my support network for a long time."

– Helen Carmody

ACKNOWLEDGMENTS

There are so many people who have had an impact on my life, so while I cannot thank all of you by name in these pages, know that I have appreciated every interaction, every experience, and every opportunity to learn and grow as a result of our time together.

Thank you from the bottom of my heart to the biggest superstars in my world: my husband Jay and children Leroy, Gracie, and Lincoln. You are my pillars of strength. Thank you for being by my side and trusting me every step of the way as I have been on this journey of discovery to have it all.

Words cannot express my gratitude for my family. You have given me life and provided me with everything I needed to get started in life.

I'm extremely grateful to my circle of loyal friends… you know how you are. You have made me feel seen, heard, loved, and appreciated. Thank you for having my back and being my sounding board. Special mention must be given to Paula Williamson and Frances Cayley; you have been the light in times when I find myself in darkness. Thank you for always being there.

Thank you to my mentors Michelle Morrison, Lisa Ware, Feda Adra, Roz White, and a few other names that are not published here. You have said the right words at the right times. Thank you for seeing me, valuing my opinions, and being strong enough to guide me so my compass is always pointing in the direction I want to go.

My team, you are so loyal, back my crazy ideas, and stand by me through thick and thin.

Thank you to *you* for being brave enough to venture off on your own journey of self-discovery. It is on this path that you will find your passion, your genius zone, and the people who will support you along the way. Just know, you *can* have it all, and don't let anyone tell you otherwise!